Richard L Campbell

Historical Sketches of Colonial Florida

Richard L Campbell

Historical Sketches of Colonial Florida

ISBN/EAN: 9783337154738

Printed in Europe, USA, Canada, Australia, Japan

Cover: Foto ©ninafisch / pixelio.de

More available books at **www.hansebooks.com**

HISTORICAL SKETCHES

—OF—

Colonial Florida.

—BY—

RICHARD L. CAMPBELL.

CLEVELAND, OHIO:
THE WILLIAMS PUBLISHING CO.
1892.

Entered according to Act of Congress, in year 1892, by RICHARD L. CAMPBELL, in the office of the Librarian of Congress, at Washington.

PREFACE.

THE inducement to write this book was to supply, in a slight measure, the want of any particular history of British rule in West Florida. With that inducement, however, the effort would not have been made but for the sources of original information existing in the Archives of the Dominion of Canada, as well as others, pointed out to me by Dr. William Kingsford of Ottawa, author of the 'History of Canada;' to whom I take this occasion of making my acknowledgments.

An account of British rule necessitated one of Spanish colonial annals, both before and after it.

If any apology be necessary for the space devoted to the Creeks, it will be found in the considerations that for twenty years the body of the nation was within the limits of British West Florida; that their relations with the British, formed during that period, influenced their conduct towards the United States until after the War of 1812; and above all, that the life of Alexander McGillivray forms a part of the history of West Florida, both under British and Spanish rule.

The prominence given to Pensacola is due to its having been the capital of both British and Spanish West Florida, and therefore the centre of provincial influence.

CONTENTS.

PAGE.

CHAPTER I... 9

The Discovery of Pensacola Bay by the Panfilo de Narvaez. The Visits of Maldonado, Captain of the Fleet of Hernando de Soto.

CHAPTER II.. 19

The Settlement of Don Tristram de Luna at Santa Maria—His Explorations—Abandonment of the Settlement—The First Pensacola.

CHAPTER III... 31

Don Andrés de Pes—Santa Maria de Galva—Don Andrés d'Arriola—The Resuscitation of Pensacola—Its Consequences.

CHAPTER IV... 36

Iberville's Expedition—Settlement at Biloxi and Mobile—Amicable Relations of the French and Spanish Colonies from 1700-1719.

CHAPTER V.. 41

War Declared by France against Spain—Bienville Surprises Metamoras—Metamoras Surprises Chateauqné—Bienville Attacks and Captures Pensacola—San Carlos and Pensacola Destroyed—Magazine Spared.

CHAPTER VI... 51

Sketch of Island Town—Its Destruction—The Third Pensacola—The Cession of Florida by Spain to Great Britain—Appearance of Town in 1763—Captain Wills' Report—Catholic Church.

CONTENTS.

CHAPTER VII... 59

British West Florida—Pensacola the Capital—Government Established—Johnstone first Governor—British Settlers—First Survey of the Town—Star Fort—Public Buildings—Resignation of Johnstone—His Successor, Monteforte Brown.

CHAPTER VIII.. 71

General Bouquet—General Haldimand.

CHAPTER IX.. 78

Governor Elliott—Social and Military Life in Pensacola—Gentlemen—Women—Fiddles—George Street—King's Wharf on November 14, 1768.

CHAPTER X... 87

Governor Peter Chester—Ft. George of the British and St. Michael of the Spanish—Council Chamber—Tartar Point—Red Cliff.

CHAPTER XI.. 93

Representative Government.

CHAPTER XII... 97

Growth of Pensacola—Panton, Leslie & Co.—A King and the Beaver—Governor Chester's Palace and Chariot—The White House of the British and Casa Blanca of the Spanish—General Gage—Commerce—Earthquake.

CHAPTER XIII..111

Military Condition of West Florida in 1778—General John Campbell—The Waldecks—Spain at War with Britain—Bute, Baton Rouge and Fort Charlotte Capitulate to Galvez—French Town—Famine in Fort George—Galvez's Expedition Against Pensacola—Solana's Fleet Enters the Harbor—Spaniards Effect a Landing—Spanish Entrenchment Surprised—The Fall of Charleston Celebrated in Fort George.

CONTENTS.

CHAPTER XIV..131

Fort San Bernardo—Siege of Fort George—Explosion of Magazine—The Capitulation—The March Through the Breach—British Troops Sail from Pensacola to Brooklyn.

CHAPTER XV...142

Political Aspect of the Capitulation—Treaty of Versailles—English Exodus—Widow of the White House.

CHAPTER XVI..150

Boundary Lines—William Panton and Spain—Indian Trade—Indian Ponies and Traders—Business of Panton, Leslie & Co.

CHAPTER XVII...158

Lineage of Alexander McGillivray—His Education—Made Grand Chief—His Connection with Milfort—His Relations with William Panton—His Administration of Creek Affairs—Appointed Colonel by the British—Treaty with Spain—Commissioned Colonel by the Spanish—Invited to New York by Washington—Treaty—Commissioned a Brigadier-General by the United States—His Sister, Sophia Durant—His Trials—His Death at Pensacola.

CHAPTER XVIII..200

Governor Folch—Barrancas—Changes in the Plan of the Town—Ship Pensacola—Disputed Boundaries—Square Ferdinand VII.—English Names of Streets Changed for Spanish Names—Palafox—Saragossa—Reding—Baylen Romana—Alcaniz—Tarragona.

CHAPTER XIX..217

Folch Leaves West Florida—His Successors—War of 1812—Tecumseh's Visit to the Seminoles and Creeks—Consequences—Fort Mims—Percy and Nicholls' Expedition.

CONTENTS.

CHAPTER XX..227

Attack on Fort Boyer by Percy and Nicholls—Jackson's March on Pensacola in 1814—The Town Captured—Percy and Nicholls Driven Out—Consequences of the War to the Creeks—Don Manuel Gonzalez.

CHAPTER XXI...243

Seminole War, 1818—Jackson Invades East Florida—Defeats the Seminoles—Captures St. Marks—Arbuthnot and Ambrister—Prophet Francis—His Daughter.

CHAPTER XXII..252

Jackson's Invasion of West Florida in 1818—Masot's Protest—Capture of Pensacola—Capitulation of San Carlos—Provisional Government Established by Jackson—Pensacola Restored to Spain—Governor Callava—Treaty of Cession—Congressional Criticism of Jackson's Conduct.

CHAPTER XXIII...267

Treaty Ratified—Jackson Appointed Provisional Governor—Goes to Pensacola—Mrs. Jackson in Pensacola—Change of Flags—Callava Imprisoned—Territorial Government—Governor Duval—First Legislature Meets at Pensacola.

ERRATA.

Page 10. *Sixteenth* for Eighteenth.
" 61. *Distant* for District.
" 113. *Journal* for Journey.
" 117. *1779* for 1789.
" 225. *Barrataria* for Banataria.
" 276. *Domingo* for Doningo.
" 233. *During* for Doing.

CHAPTER I.

The Discovery of Pensacola Bay by Panfilo de Narvaez—
The Visits of Maldonado, Captain of the Fleet of
Hernando de Soto.

ON ONE of the early days of October, 1528, there could have been seen, coasting westward along and afterwards landing on the south shore of Santa Rosa Island, five small, rudely-constructed vessels, having for sails a grotesque patchwork of masculine under and over-wear. That fleet was the fruit of the first effort at naval construction within the present limits of the United States. It was built of yellow pine and caulked with palmetto fibre and pitch. Horses' tails and manes furnished the cordage, as did their hides its water vessels. Its freightage consisted of two hundred and forty human bodies, wasted and worn by fatigue and exposure, and as many hearts heavy and racked with disappointment. It was commanded by His

Excellency Panfilo de Narvaez, Captain-general and Adelantado of Florida, a tall, big-limbed, red-haired, one-eyed man, "with a voice deep and sonorous as though it came from a cavern."

These were the first white men to make footprints on the shores of Pensacola Bay and to look out upon its waters. Although they landed on the Island, there is no evidence that their vessels entered the harbor.

Narvaez, an Hidalgo, born at Valladolid about 1480, was a man capable of conceiving and undertaking great enterprises, but too rash and ill-starred for their successful execution, possessing the ambition and avarice which impelled the Spanish adventurers to the shores of the Gulf of Mexico during the eighteenth century, with whom Indian life was but a trifling sacrifice for a pearl or an ounce of gold.

Five years before his Florida expedition he had been appointed, with a large naval and land force under his command, by Velasquez, governor of Cuba, to supersede Cortez, the conqueror of Mexico, and to send him in chains to Havana, to answer charges of insubordination to the authority of Velasquez. But Cortez was not the man to be thus superseded. Never did his genius for great enterprises make a more striking display than by the measures he adopted and executed in this emergency. By them he converted that threatening expedition into one of succor for himself, embracing every supply, soldiers included, he required to complete his conquests. Of this great achievement the defeat of the incompetent Narvaez was only an incident.

No labored comparison of conqueror and vanquished could present a more striking contrast between them than that suggested by their first interview. "Esteem it," said Narvaez, "great good fortune that you have taken me captive." "It is the least of the things I have done in Mexico," replied Cortez, a sarcasm aimed at the incapacity of Narvaez, apart from the gains of the victor.

The fruits of the expedition to Narvaez were the loss of his left eye, shackles, imprisonment, banishment, and the humiliation of kneeling to his conqueror and attempting to kiss his hand. To the Aztec the result was the introduction of a scourge that no surrender could placate, no submission, however absolute and abject, could stay, and, therefore, more pitiless than the sword of Cortez—the small-pox.

After leaving Mexico, Narvaez appeared before the Emperor Charles V., to accuse Cortez of treason, and to petition for a redress of his own wrongs, but the dazzling success of Cortez, to say nothing of his large remittances to the royal treasury, was an effectual answer to every charge. The emperor, however, healed the wounded pride, and silenced the complaints of the prosecutor by a commission with the aforementioned sonorous titles to organize an expedition for a new conquest, by which he might compensate himself for the loss of the treasures and empire of Montezuma, which he had so disastrously failed to snatch from the iron grasp of Cortez.

The preparations to execute this commission having been made by providing a fleet, a land force, consisting of men-at-arms and cavalry, as well as the necessary supplies, Narvaez, in April, 1528, sailed for the Florida coast, and landed at or near Tampa bay.

Having resolved on a westward movement,

he ordered his fleet to sail along the coast, whilst he, by rather a circuitous march, would advance in the same direction. This parting was at once final and fatal. He again reached the Gulf, somewhere in the neighborbood of St. Marks, with his command woefully wasted and diminished by toil, battle and disease; and, as can well be imagined, with his dreams of avarice and dominion rudely dispelled.

No tidings of the fleet from which he had so lucklessly parted being obtainable, despair improvised that fleet with motley sails which we have seen mooring off the island of Santa Rosa in the early days of October, its destination being Mexico—a destination, however, which was but another delusion that the winds and the waves were to dispel.

Narvaez found a grave in the maw of the sea, as did most of the remnant of his followers. Famine swept off others, leaving only four to reach Mexico after a land journey requiring years, marked by perils and sufferings incident to such a journey through a vast forest bounded only by the sea, intersected by great rivers, inhabited by savages, and infested by wild beasts.

One of the survivors was Cabeça de Vaca, the treasurer and historian of the expedition.

Twelve years elapsed after Narvaez discovered Pensacola Bay before the shadow of the white man's sail again fell upon its waters. In January, 1540, Capitano Maldonado, who was the commander of the fleet which brought Fernando de Soto to the Florida coast, entered the harbor, gave it a careful examination, and bestowed upon it the name of Puerta d'Anchusi, a name probably suggested by Ochus,* which it bore at the time of his visit. In entering Ochus he ended a voyage westward, made in search of a good harbor, under the orders of Soto, who was at that time somewhere on the Forida coast to the westward of Apalachee.

Having returned to Soto, Maldonado made so favorable a report—the first official report—of the advantages of Puerta d' Anchusi that Soto determined to make it his base of supply. He accordingly ordered Maldonado to proceed to Havana, and after having procured the

---

* So the name is given by historians; but, to be consistent with the termination of other Indian names in West Florida, it should be written Ochee or Ochusee.

required succors to sail to Puerta d' Anchusi, where he intended to go himself, and there to await Maldonado's return before he ventured into the interior; a prudent resolve, suggested possibly by the sight of the bones of Narvaez's horses, which had been slain to furnish cordage and water-vessels for his fleet.

But the resolve was as brief as it was wise. A few days after Maldonado's departure a captured Indian so beguiled Soto with tales of gold to be found far to the northeast of Apalachee, where he then was, that banishing all thoughts of Puerta d' Anchusi from his mind, he began that circuitious march which carried him into South Carolina, northern Georgia, and Alabama, where he wandered in search of treasure until disappointment, wasted forces, and needed supplies again turned his march southward, and his thoughts to his rendezvous with Maldonado.

That rendezvous was to be in October, 1540. Faithful to instructions, Maldonado was at Puerta d' Anchusi at the appointed time with a fleet bearing all the required supplies. But Soto did not keep the tryst. He was then at Mauvilla, or Maubila, supposed to be Choctaw

Bluff, on the Alabama river, absorbed by difficulties and engaged in conflicts such as he had never before encountered. Through Indians they had communicated, and intense was the satisfaction of Soto and his command at the prospect of a relief of their wants, repose from their toils, and tidings of their friends and loved ones.

Soto, however, still ambitious of emulating the achievements of Cortez and Pizzaro, looked upon Puerta d' Anchusi as only a base of supply and refuge for temporary repose, from which again to set out in search of his goal. But very different were the views of his followers. By eaves-dropping on a dark night behind their tents, he learned that to them Puerta d' Anchusi was not to be a haven of temporary rest only, but the first stage of their journey homeward, where Soto and his fortunes were to be abandoned.

This information again banished Puerta d' Anchusi from his thoughts under the promptings of pride, which impelled him to prefer death in the wilderness to the mockery and humiliation of failure. He at once resolved to march deeper into the heart of the continent, and, unconsciously, nearer to the mighty river in whose cold bosom he was to find a grave.

As in idea we go into the camp at Mauvilla, on the morning when the word of command was given for a westward march, we see depicted on the war-worn visages of that iron band naught but gloom and disappointment, as, constrained by the stern will of one man, they obediently fall into ranks without a murmur, much less a sign of revolt.

Again, if in fancy we stand on the deck of Maldonado's ship at Puerta d' Anchusi, we may realize the keen watchfulness and the deep anxiety with which day after day and night after night he scans the shore and hills beyond to catch a glint of spear or shield, or strains his ear to hear a bugle note announcing the approach of his brothers-in-arms. And only after long, weary months was the vigil ended, as he weighed anchor and sailed out of the harbor to go to other points on the Gulf shore where happily he might yet meet and succor his commander.

To this task did he devote himself for three

years, scouring the Gulf coast from Florida to Vera Cruz, until the curtain of the drama was lifted for him, to find that seventeen months previously his long-sought chief had been lying in the depths of the Mississippi, and that a wretched remnant only of that proud host, which he had last seen in glittering armor on the coast of Florida, had reached Mexico after undergoing indescribable perils and privations.

CHAPTER II.

The Settlement of Don Tristram de Luna at Santa Maria—His Explorations—Abandonment of the Settlement—The First Pensacola.

NEARLY twenty years passed away after Maldonado's visit to Ochus before Europeans again looked upon its shores.

In 1556, the viceroy of Mexico, and the bishop of Cuba united in a memorial to the Emperor Charles V. representing Florida as an inviting field for conquest and religious work. Imperial sanction having been secured, an expedition was organized under the command of Don Tristram de Luna to effect the triple objects of bringing gold into the emperor's treasury, extending his dominions, and enlarging the bounds of the spiritual kingdom by winning souls to the church. For the first two enterprises one thousand five hundred soldiers were provided, and for the last a host of ecclesiastics, friars, and other spiritual teachers. Puerta d' Anchusi was selected as the place of the projected settlement, the base from which the cross and the sword were to advance to their respective conquests.

Accordingly, on the fourteenth day of August, 1559, de Luna's fleet cast anchor within the harbor, which he named Santa Maria; the same year in which the monarch who authorized the expedition died, the month, and nearly the day on which he, a living man, was engaged in the paradoxical farce of participating in his own funeral ceremonies in the monastery of Yusté.

The population of two thousand souls, which the fleet brought, with the required supplies of every kind, having been landed, the work of settlement began. Of the place where the settlement was made there exists no historic information, and we are left to the inference that the local advantages which afterwards induced d' Arriola to select what is now called Barrancas as the site of his town, governed the selection of de Luna's, unless tradition enables us to identify the spot, as a future page will endeavor to do.

The destruction of the fleet by a hurricane

within a week after its arrival threw a shadow over the infant settlement, aggravating the natural discontent incident to all colonizations, resulting from the contrast between the stern realities of experience and of expectations colored by the imagination of the colonist. Against that discontent, ever on the increase, de Luna manfully and successfully struggled until 1562; and thus it was, that for two years and more there existed a town of about two thousand inhabitants on the shores of Pensacola Bay, which antedated by four years St. Augustine, the oldest town of the United States.

Don Tristram de Luna sent expeditions into the interior, and finally led one in person. In these journeys the priest and the friar joined, and daily in a tabernacle of tree boughs the holy offices of the Catholic faith were performed, the morning chant and the evening hymn breaking the silence and awakening the echoes of the primeval forest.

Where they actually went, and how far north, it is impossible to say, owing to our inability to identify the sites of villages, rivers, and other land marks mentioned in the narratives of their journeys. The presumption is strong, however, that they took, and followed northward the Indian trail, on the ridge beginning at Pensacola Bay, forming the water shed between the Perdido and Escambia rivers, and beyond their headwaters uniting with the elevated country which throws off its springs and creeks eastward to the Chattahoochee and westward to the Alabama and Tallapoosa rivers. It continued northerly to the Tennessee river; a lateral trail diverging to where the city of Montgomery now stands, and thence to the site of Wetumpka; and still another leading to what is now Grey's Ferry on the Tallapoosa.

That trail, according to tradition, was the one by which the Indians, from the earliest times, passed between the Coosa country and the sea, the one followed in later times by the Indian traders on their pack-ponies, and the line of march of General Jackson in his invasion of Florida in 1814.

That it was regarded and used as their guiding thread by de Luna's expeditions in penetrating the unknown country north of Santa Maria they sought to explore, is evidenced by two facts. They came to a large river which, instead of crossing, they followed its course, undoubtedly by the ridge, and, therefore, not far from the trail. They also came to or crossed the line of de Soto's march, which he had made ten years previously, as following the trail they would be compelled to do and found amongst the Indians a vivid recollection of the destruction and rapine of their people by white men, which they assigned as the cause of the then sparsity of population, and the abandonment of clearings formerly under cultivation

So impressed was de Luna with the fertility and other attractive features of the beautiful region of Central Alabama, which he explored, that he determined to plant a colony there. But in that design he was eventually thwarted by the discontent and insubordination of his followers, the most of whom, from the first, seem to have had no other object in view than to break up the settlement, and to terminate their insupportable exile by returning to Mexico.

There were amongst those composing the expedition two elements which proved fatal to its success. The gold-greedy soon found that the pine barrens of Florida, and the fertile valleys of Alabama were not the eldorado of which they had dreamed. To the friar, the spiritual outlook was not more promising, the Indians he encountered being more ready to scalp their would-be spiritual guide than to open their ears to his teachings.

Ostensibly, to procure supplies for the colony, two friars sailed for Havana and thence to Vera Cruz, to make known its necessities to the Viceroy of Mexico, and solicit the required succor. But, as soon as they could reach his ear they endeavored to persuade him of the futility of the expedition, and the unpromising character of the country as a field for colonization.

At first, his heart being in the enterprise, he was loathe to listen to reports so inconsistent with the glowing accounts which had prompted the expedition and enlisted his zealous support; but, at last, an impression was made upon him, and an inquiry resolved upon.

But the viceroyal investigation was forestalled by the visit to Santa Maria of Don Angel de Villafana, whom the Viceroy of Cuba had appointed governor of that, at that time undefined region called Florida, who permitted the dissatisfied colonists to embark in his vessels, and abandon the, to them, hateful country in which they had passed two miserable years.

Don Tristram de Luna, with a few followers only, remained, with the fixed resolution to maintain the settlement, provided he could secure the approbation and assistance of the Viceroy. But an application for that purpose, accompanied by representations of the inviting character of the interior for settlement, was met by a prompt recall of de Luna and an order for the abandonment of the enterprise.

Don Tristram, against whom history makes no accusations of cruelty or bloodshed during his expeditions into the interior, or his stay at Santa Maria, and who, animated by the spirit of legitimate colonization, sought only to found a new settlement, invites respect, if not admiration, as a character distinct and apart from the gold-seeking cut-throat adventurers that Spain sent in shoals to the Gulf shores during the sixteenth century. Sympathy with him in his trials and regret at his failure, induce the reflection that, perhaps, had he been burdened with fewer gold-seekers and only one-twentieth of the ecclesiastics who encumbered and leavened the colony with discontent, his settlement might have proved permanent.

The local results of de Luna's expedition were fixing, for a time, the name of Santa Maria upon the Bay, and permanently stamping upon its shores the name Pensacola; and here narration must be suspended to determine the origin of the latter.

Roberts says, the name was "that of an Indian tribe inhabiting round the bay but which was destroyed." Mr. Fairbanks tells us it was "a name derived from the locality having been, formerly, that of the town of a tribe of Indians called Pencacolas, which had been entirely exterminated in conflicts with neighboring tribes."

The first objection to this assigned origin of the name is, that it is evidently not Indian, such names in West Florida invariably terminating with a double e, as for examples, Apalachee, Choctawhatchee, Uchee, Ochusee, Escambee, Ochesee, Chattahoochee. The "cola" added to

Apalachee, and "ia" substituted in Escambia for ee, indicate the difference between the terminations of Indian and Spanish names.

Again, amongst savages, we should expect to find in the name of a place an indication of a natural object, the name being expressive of the object, and hence as lasting. But, that the accident of an encampment of savages upon a locality should stamp that locality with their tribal name, as a designation that should survive not only the encampment, but the very existence of the tribe, is incredible. An extinct tribe would in a generation or two cease to have a place in the traditions of surviving tribes, because their extinction would be only an ordinary event amongst American savages.

The termination being Spanish, and no natural object existing suggestive of the name, we naturally turn our search to a vocabulary of Spanish names, historical and geographical.

Perched upon a rock springing 240 feet high from the Mediterranean shore of Spain, connected with the mainland by a narrow strip of sand, is the fortified little seaport of Peniscola. Substitute "a" for "i," transpose "s" and we have the name for the original of which we seek. The seaports of Spain furnished the great body of Spanish adventurers to America in the sixteenth and seventeenth centuries; and what more likely than that some native of the little town crowning with its vine-clad cottages the huge rock that looks out upon the "midland ocean," should have sought to honor his home by fixing its name upon a spot in the new world?

When and by whom the name was affixed to our shores is an interesting inquiry. Neither Roberts, nor Fairbanks, nor any other authority, informs us. It comes into history with the advent of d' Arriola, whose settlement will be the subject of a future page.

Three hypotheses furnish as many answers to the question: it was original with Arriola to the extent at least of a new application of a Spanish name; or he found the place already named in some chart or document now lost to us; or already fixed by an Indian tradition, according to Roberts and Fairbanks.

The first hypothesis requires no comment. The second rests upon the existence of a fact of which we can procure no evidence. The third is a tradition founded upon, or involving, a Spanish name.

Very extraordinary events or striking objects only are the subjects of the traditions of savage tribes; and what event can be imagined more extraordinary and impressive to the savage mind than to be brought suddenly in contact, for the first time, with the white man under all the circumstances and conditions of de Luna's settlement? It was one not likely to pass out of tradition in the lapse of one hundred and thirty-three years, for two long lives only would be required for its transmission. The settlers would be, in Indian terminology, a tribe; their departure would be an extinction; and vanity would at last attribute its ending to the prowess of the Red man.

A name that identifies a locality and forms a feature of a purely Indian tradition, having no reference to or connection whatever with the white man, must be an Indian name. Here, however, the name under discussion is a Spanish and not an Indian name. The conclusion is, therefore, irresistible, that as the name is

Spanish the tradition relates to Spaniards, and that the former is a Spanish designation of the locality of the people to whom it relates.

The settlement of de Luna was the only Spanish settlement with which the Indians could have come in contact before Arriola's. That settlement, therefore, must be the subject of the Indian tradition, and the Spanish name Pensacola must have been its name.

CHAPTER III.

Don Andrés de **Pes**—**Santa Maria** de Galva—Don Andrés d' Arriola—The Resuscitation of Pensacola—Its Consequences.

In 1693, Don Andrés de Pes entered the Bay, but how long he remained, or why he came, whether for examination of its advantages, from curiosity, or necessity, to disturb its solitude and oblivion of one hundred and thirty-three years, history does not say. But as a memorial of his visit, he supplemented the name de Luna had given it with de Galva, in honor of the Viceroy of Mexico; and thus, it comes into colonial history with the long title of Santa Maria de Galva.

In 1696, three years after de Pes' visit, Don Andrés d' Arriola, with three hundred soldiers and settlers, took formal possession of the harbor and the surrounding country, which, to make effectual and permanent, he built a "square fort with bastions" at what is now called Barrancas, which he named San Carlos. As the beginning, or rather reconstruction of a town named Pensacola, he erected some houses adjacent to the fort. And there, too, was built a church, historically the first ever erected on the shores of Pensacola Bay, but presumptively the second; for it is hardly credible that the large settlement of de Luna, embracing so many ecclesiastics, should have failed to observe the universal custom of the Spaniards to build a church wherever they planted a colony. Irresistible, therefore, is the inference that the first notes of a church-bell heard within the limits of the United States were those which rolled over the waters of Pensacola Bay and the white hills of Santa Rosa from 1559 to 1562.

Having demonstrated that the settlement of de Luna was the original Pensacola, that of Arriola was apparently the second, though actually but a resuscitation of the colony of 1559; for the name, the people, though not the same generation, and the place being one, mere lapse of time should not be permitted to destroy the unity which may be so justly attributed to the two settlements.

The inhabitants of the town having been largely recruited by malefactors banished from Mexico, must be notched low in the scale of morals. But, perhaps, in some instances at least, actions were then adjudged crimes deserving banishment which might be deemed virtues in a more enlightened age, and under free institutions; for under the despotic colonial governments of Spanish America in that age to criticize the vices, or censure the lawless edicts of a satrap, was a heinous offence, for which transportation was but a mild punishment.

Originally, Spain's dominion was asserted over the entire circle of the shores of the Gulf of Mexico, as well as over all the islands which they girdled. But upon the voyage of La Salle from the upper waters of the Mississippi to the sea, France asserted a claim, under the name of Louisiana, to the entire valley of the river from its spring-heads to the Gulf, making to the extent of the southern limit of her claim, from east to west, a huge gap in Spain's North American empire.

But where were the eastern boundary of Louisiana, and the western limit of Florida to be fixed? Had the French expedition under Iberville reached Florida before Arriola's, Pensacola would have been included in Louisiana, and afterwards in the State of Alabama. But Arriola's settlement was first, in point of time; and it is to him must be attributed the establishment of the Perdido as the boundary line between the French and Spanish colonies, and the consequent exclusion of Pensacola from the limits of the great State of Alabama, her political influence, her fostering care, and, comparatively, from the vitalizing influence of her vast mineral and agricultural resources.

The interest of history consists not in the mere knowledge or contemplation of events as isolated facts, but in studying their inter-relations, and following their threads of connection through all the meshes of cause and effect. It is, therefore, an interesting reflection that the settlement of Arriola may not have been the absolute, though it was the apparent, cause of the consequences above pointed out. Behind it, in the shadow of a century and a third, may perchance be discerned the ultimate and final cause of those consequences in the settlement of de Luna. He planted the first colony, and because he so did, Arriola settled his on that spot upon which the lost chart and tradition probably coincided in fixing the Pensacola of 1559.

How illustrative of the truth that as one human life can have but one beginning, so it is with that aggregate of human lives which we call a people. "In the almighty hands of eternal God, a people's history is interrupted and recommenced—never."*

---

* The last sentence of Guizot's History of France.

CHAPTER IV.

Iberville's Expedition—Settlement at Biloxi and Mobile—Amicable Relations of the French and Spanish Colonies from 1700-1719.

THE French expedition referred to in the previous chapter, the delay of which was so fateful to the growth and commercial future of Pensacola, appeared off the mouth of the harbor in January, 1699. But, observing the Spanish flag flying from the mast-head of two war vessels lying in the Bay and from the flagstaff of Fort San Carlos, they did not enter the harbor, but cast anchor off the Island of Santa Rosa. Thence an application was made to the Spanish governor for permission to enter, which was promptly refused.

After that curt refusal of the Spaniards, the fleet, consisting of three vessels under the command of Lemoine d' Iberville, accompanied by his brothers, Bienvielle and Sauville, which was taking out a colony with the necessary supplies to settle southern Louisiana, sailed westward and took formal possession of the country west of the Perdido river.

Iberville's first settlement was made at Biloxi on the twenty-seventh of February, 1699, but it was afterwards abandoned, in 1702, and removed to Mobile.

To the accession of Philip V., a Bourbon prince, to the Spanish crown, whilst Louis XIV. reigned in France, must be attributed the strangely peaceful settlement of the Perdido as the boundary line between Louisiana and Florida. For the politic, if not natural, harmony existing between two kings belonging to the same royal family, a grandfather and a grandson, both the objects of jealousy and suspicion to the other nations of Europe, necessarily inspired a like feeling in their respective colonial officers. Hence it was that we find that the ineffectual expedition of Governor Ravolli of Pensacola, in 1700, to expel the French from Ship Island, was the last instance of hostility between the Louisiana French and the Florida Spaniards for a period of nineteen years.

Indeed, so intimate were the relations between the two colonies, that Iberville, coming from France, in 1702, with two war ships taking succor to the French colonists, terminated their voyage at Pensacola, and thence sent the supplies to Mobile in small vessels. Again, in 1703, he began a voyage to France by sailing from Pensacola.

The War of the Spanish Succession, in which England was the antagonist of Spain and France, tightened the bonds of amity between the colonies of the latter. In 1702, in anticipation of an English expedition against Pensacola, Governor Martino readily procured from Bienville a needed supply of arms and ammunition. On the other hand, in 1704, Governor Martino promptly furnished food from his stores at Pensacola to the famine-threatened colonists at Mobile; that kind office being a just requital of a like humanity which had been exercised by Bienville, in 1702, towards the starving garrison of San Carlos.

In 1706-7, eighteen Englishmen from Carolina, heading a large body of Indians, made inroads upon the Spanish settlements in Florida, and, strange as it may seem, extended their operations as far westward as Pensacola. In the latter year, Bienville was applied to by the Spanish governor to aid him in defending Pensacola from an impending attack by the Englishmen and their Indian allies. Prompt and bold in action, Bienville at once advanced from Mobile with one hundred and twenty Canadians to assist the Spaniards. But no conflict occurred, for after a few days of hostile demonstrations the enemy abandoned their enterprise, owing to the want of necessary supplies.

In other ways, too, the good feeling and intimate relations of the two colonies were manifested. We learn, from a letter of the mean, jealous, and growling Governor Condillac of Louisiana to Count Pontchartrain, that, in 1713, there existed a trade between Pensacola and Mobile, in which the former was supplied by the latter with lumber, poultry and vegetables—a petty traffic, but not too small to excite the jealousy of the old grumbler.

Such were the friendly relations existing between the Florida Spaniards and the Louisiana French up to 1719, being the year after

Bienville had founded the city of New Orleans; relations which must be borne in mind to enable us to form an enlightened judgment upon the actions of the men engaged in the bloody drama which was ushered in by the nineteen years of kind offices and good fellowship which have been mentioned.

Lemoine d' Iberville, a Canadian, esteemed the most skillful officer of the French navy brilliantly distinguished on many occasions, was selected to command the expedition to southern Louisiana, designed to perfect by colonization the claim France founded upon the voyage of La Salle. He and his brothers, Bienville, the founder of New Orleans, Sauville, Sevigny and Chateaugné presented a group of men seldom accorded to one family.

During a visit to Havana, d' Iberville died on the ninth of July, 1706, leaving to his brothers the task of perfecting the great enterprise to which the last seven years of his own life had been devoted.

CHAPTER V.

War Declared by France against Spain—Bienville Surprises Metamoras—Metamoras Surprises Chateaugné—Bienville Attacks and Captures Pensacola—San Carlos and Pensacola Destroyed—Magazine Spared.

ON THE thirteenth of April, 1719, two French vessels brought to the French colony the intelligence that in the previous December, France had declared war against Spain; an event of which Don Juan Pedro Metamoras, governor of Pensacola, who had just succeded Don Gregorio de Salinas, had no information.

Bienville at once organized, with all possible secrecy, an expedition by land and water to capture Pensacola by surprise. The land force, consisting of four hundred Indians and a body of Canadians, was collected at Mobile. The naval force, composed of three vessels, two of them, the *Philippe* and the *Toulouse*, carrying twenty-four guns each, under the command of Sevigny, had its rendezvous at Dauphin Island.

The movement of Bienville, who marched across the country with his land force, and that of the fleet were so well timed that on the fourteenth of May, at 5 o'clock in the afternoon, as the vessels presented their shotted broadsides to San Carlos, Bienville, his Canadians, and Indians, appeared on its land side. There was, of course, nothing for Metamoras to do but to order the chamade to be beaten and to settle the terms of capitulation. He surrendered the post and all public property within his jurisdiction. It was stipulated that he and his garrison should march out of the fort with the honors of war, retaining a cannon and three charges of powder, that they should be transported to Havana in French vessels, that the town should be protected from violence, and that the property of the soldiers and that of the inhabitants should be respected.

The victim of such a ruse, it was natural that Metamoras should have directed his thoughts to retaliation; and it is probable that during the voyage to Havana he meditated for his captors a surprise as complete and prompt as that which he had just suffered from them.

After the French vessels, the *Toulouse* and the *Mareschal de Villars* had reached Cuba and landed their prisoners, they were seized by order of the governor of Havana, who had at once, upon learning of the disaster at Pensacola, determined upon its prompt reparation by a recapture. He accordingly prepared a fleet, consisting of a Spanish war ship, nine brigantines and the two French vessels. In this fleet Metamoras and his lately captured troops, besides others, embarked for Pensacola.

On the sixth of August, the Spanish fleet was off the harbor. The two French vessels, flying the French flag, first entered as decoys, to enable them to secure favorable positions for attacking San Carlos in the event of a refusal to surrender. Immediately after them came the Spanish war vessel. The ruse for position succeeded, but the demand to surrender was peremptorily refused by Chateaugné, the commander of the fort. To an almost harmless cannonade there succeeded an armistice, which the French sought to have extended to four, but which the Spaniards limited to two days.

After the expiration of the armistice, another

ineffectual exchange of cannon shots was followed by the surrender of the fort; the terms being that the garrison of one hundred and sixty men should march out with the honors of war and be sent to Havana as prisoners. Chateaugné also was to be sent there and thence to Spain to await exchange. They were accordingly all taken to Havana. Chateaugné, however, instead of being sent from there to Spain, was imprisoned in Moro Castle, where he remained only a short time, in consequence of the energetic preparations which his brother, Bienville, was then making for his deliverance.

Metamoras, once again in command at Pensacola, fully realized that the stake for which he and Bienville had been playing was not to be finally won by such strategems, as each in turn had been the other's victim, and that the two which had been achieved were but preludes to a trial by battle. Appreciating, too, the bold, prompt and enterprising Bienville, he well calculated that his time for preparation would be short, and he accordingly improved it to the best of his abilities and resources.

He erected a battery on Point Seguenza, the

western extremity of Santa Rosa Island, which he named Principe d' Asturias, to aid San Carlos and the Spanish fleet in resisting an attack by sea. To guard San Carlos from a land attack, he built a stockade in its rear. To man all his works he had a force of six hundred men.

The Fort was captured by Metamoras early in August, and on the eighteenth of the following September Bienville was ready to settle by arms his right to retain it.

The celerity of Bieneville's preparations was due, however, to the accidental arrival at Dauphin Island of a French fleet under Champmeslin, who at once relieved him from the care and preparation of the seaward operations of his expedition.

The naval force of the French consisted of six vessels, under the command of Champmeslin, the *Hercules* of sixty-four guns, the *Mars* of sixty, the *Triton* of fifty, the *Union* of thirty-six, the —— of thirty-six and the *Philippe* of twenty. The land force, commanded by Bienville in person, consisted of two hundred and fifty troops lately arrived from France, besides a large number of

Canadian volunteers, which, when it reached Perdido, was joined by five hundred Indians under Longueville.

Whilst Bienville was moving towards Pensacola, Champmeslin, having sailed from Dauphin Island, entered the harbor on the eighteenth of September with five of his vessels, and was soon engaged in a fierce conflict with Principe d' Asturias, the Spanish fleet, and San Carlos. At the time the five vessels went into action, it was supposed that the *Hercules* was following them, but her commander hesitated to cross the bar, owing to her draught of twenty-one feet, a hesitation which almost proved fatal to her consorts, for, relying upon the support of her heavy batteries, they now found themselves without it, whilst they were under the concentrated fire of the Spanish fleet and the two forts.

In that conjuncture, however, they were saved by one of those inspirations which sometimes come to a man in the supreme hour of trial, making him for the occasion the soul of a host. A Canadian pilot, being inspired himself, inspired the commander of the *Hercules* with confidence in his ability to take her over the bar and into the action. With a cheer from her crew and all the canvas she could bear, the gallant ship sped under the guidance of the bold Canadian to the rescue of her consorts.

Speedily her sixty-four guns turned the tide of battle. Whilst her heavy broadside of thirty-two guns soon battered Principe d' Asturias into silence, her consorts poured their fire into the Spanish fleet, which, now short of powder, struck its colors.

After a conflict of two hours, San Carlos was the only point of defense left to the Spaniards, and that too, threatened by a new foe. Bienville was in its rear ready for an assault, which he soon boldly made. He was, however, so much impeded by the stockade that he withdrew his men until he could be better prepared for another attack. In the assault, it is said, his Indian allies emulated the French soldiers in daring and in their efforts to tear away the impeding stockade. But their war-whoop was more effectual and decisive than their valor. Impressing the Spaniards, as it did, with visions of blood-dripping scalps, it disposed them to obviate by surrender the dire consequences of a successful assault, for they felt that Bienville, however so disposed, would be powerless to stay the Indian's scalping knife when his blood was at battle heat. Accordingly, before the assault was repeated, Metamoras signaled for a parley, which resulted not in a capitulation on terms which he asked for, but in a surrender at discretion.

Even after the cooling process of the time required for the parley and arranging the surrender, the Indians were so loath to forego their scalping pastime, the precious boon of victory, that it was necessary for Bienville to redeem the scalps of the Spaniards by bestowing one-half of their effects upon his allies, and reserving the other half only for his own soldiers.

When Don Alphonso, the commander of the Spanish fleet, surrendered his sword to Champmeslin, the latter returned it with the complimentary assurance that the Don was worthy to wear it. But Bienville would not even condescend to accept that of Metamoras, but directed him to deliver it to a by-standing soldier.

But the real hero of this battle, like the real

heroes of many other fields of glory, must be unnamed, for though it is recorded that the pilot of the *Hercules* was rewarded with a patent of nobility for his skill and daring, there is no accessible record of his name.

Having won a surrender at discretion, it was Bienville's pleasure to send Metamoras and a sufficient number of Spanish troops to Havana, in a Spanish vessel, to be exchanged for the Frenchmen who had been sent there in August; and thus it was that he worked the deliverance of his brother Chateaugné from his imprisonment in Mora Castle. The rest of the Spaniards were sent to France as prisoners of war.

It was his will and pleasure likewise to burn the town of Pensacola, and to utterly destroy San Carlos by blowing it up with powder. The only structure left undestroyed was the magazine which stood about half a mile from the fort.

Upon the ruins of San Carlos there was fixed a tablet announcing: "In the year 1718, on the eighteenth day of September, Monsieur Desnard de Champmeslin, Commander of His

Most Christian Majesty, captured this place and the Island of Santa Rosa by force of arms."

Thus did the Pensacola of Arriola, after having been a shuttlecock in the cruel game of war —captured, recaptured and captured again within four months — perish utterly in the throes of a convulsion and the glare of a conflagration; a fate which may be traced to the intrigues of Cardinal Alberoni, the ambitious and crafty minister of Philip V., resulting in a war in which Spain, without an ally, was confronted by the united arms of France, Great Britain, Holland and Austria. "I quickened a corpse" was the vain boast by which he expressed the change he had effected in Spanish policy, one of the many disastrous consequences of which was the ending in fire and blood of a little settlement on the far-off shores of the new world.

CHAPTER VI.

Sketch of Island Town—Its Destruction—The Third Pensacola—The Cession of Florida by Spain to Great Britain—Appearance of Town in 1763—Captain Wills' Report—Catholic Church.

On February 17, 1720, five months after the destruction of Pensacola, a treaty of peace between France and Spain was signed. But it was not until early in January, 1723, that Bienville, under orders from the French government, formally restored Pensacola to the Spaniards, or rather its site and surroundings.

Of the first settlement of the Island town there exists no account, but it is probable it began immediately after the destruction of the Pensacola of Arriola. Its origin may be accounted for by the natural precaution of Governor Metamoras upon his recapture of that place and preparation for a struggle with the French, to remove the non-combatants to a place of safety, or rather the safest in the vicinity, and there was none possessing such great advantages as Santa Rosa island. It was a narrow, uninhabited strip of land, separated from the main land in its western portion by three miles of water, rendering a settlement there comparatively free from the danger of surprise by the Indians. The deepest water for landing on the bay-side, and a supply of fresh water obtainable by digging wells, would naturally determine the location of the settlement; and these conditions were met by a place about two miles from the western point of the island, not far from the present bay-wharf of the life-saving station.

The progress the settlement made in the course of a quarter of a century is presented by the annexed engraving, which is taken from a sketch made in 1743. The artist, Don Serres, who was a resident during that year, came there in the service of the Havana Company in a schooner with a cargo for the town.

He paid New Orleans a visit, and did some profitable trading there with six thousand dollars which he had at his command. He also

A NORTH VIEW OF PENSACOLA ON THE I
1—The Fort.   2—The Church.   3—The Govenor's Hous

) OF SANTA ROSA.—DRAWN BY DOM SERRES.

secured a quantity of pitch and turpentine for his Company, as well as two pine spars, each eighty-four feet long, which he sent to Havana in the schooner. This was the beginning of the timber trade of Pensacola, its first known business transaction with New Orleans, and the last authenticated instance of one of its timber dealers engaging in the elegant pastime of sketching.

In vain has information been sought of its progress during the period between the time Don Serres made the sketch and 1754, which embraced the last eleven years of its existence, for in that year it was destroyed, together with many of its people, by a terrific hurricane. And thus it was that, as the Pensacola of Arriola perished in the conflict of human passions, its offspring was destroyed in a war of the elements.

The survivors, removing to the north shore of the Bay, settled upon a crescent-shaped body of dry land, about the eighth of a mile wide in its widest part, formed by the Bay and a titi swamp, which, extending from the mouth of an estuary on the west, curved landward to a marsh just below the outlet of another on the east. These estuaries, though seemingly the outlets of two, were in fact those of one and the same stream flowing through the swamp, and navigable by canoes for some distance from the bay. The bay-shore also curved deeply, the indentation being in fact the remnant of a cove, which, as old maps show, extended to and beyond the northern edge of the swamp.

That settlement was but a removal of Pensacola to its present site, like that by which it was removed to the island. Each settlement, in its order of time, like d'Arriola's town, being a continuation of the Pensacola founded by de Luna in 1559, four years before Menendez founded St. Augustine.

Of the history of the present Pensacola, beyond its bare existence, from 1754 to 1763, we have no information further than that its insignificance shielded it from the trials and sufferings of the seven years war ended by the treaty of Paris, February 10, 1763.

By that treaty Florida became a British colony. On July 6 of that year Captain Wills, in command of the third battery of Royal

Artillery, then at Havana, forming a part of the British force which had captured the city during the late war, was ordered by General Keppel to proceed with his command to Pensacola for the purpose of taking possession of the place. Arriving there on the seventh of August, Captain Wills having presented the order of the king of Spain to the Spanish commander for the surrender of the post, it was promptly obeyed.

It was the duty of Spain under the treaty to remove her troops from Pensacola. Her subjects, however, were, under the Ninteenth article, entitled to remain in the full enjoyment of their personal rights, religion and property; but, resolving to remove to Mexico, they applied to the Spanish government for transportation, which was promptly promised. Accordingly, on September 2, transports for the removal of the garrison and people arrived; and, on the third, the Spanish troops and the entire population, to the last man, woman and child, sailed for Vera Cruz, leaving Captain Wills and his command the only occupants of the town.

It is to a report written by him a few days after the Spanish exodus that we owe all the information we possess of the character and appearance of the town at that time.

It consisted of "40 huts, thatched with palmetto leaves, and barracks for a small garrison, the whole surrounded by a stockade of pine posts."

The report says: "The country, from the insuperable laziness of the Spaniards, still remains uncultivated. The woods are still near the village, and a few paltry gardens show the only improvements. Stock, they have none, being entirely supplied by Mobile, which is pretty well cultivated and produces sufficient for export."

Of the Indians we are presented with the following glimpse: "The Indians are numerous around. We had within a few days a visit from about two hundred of five different nations. I was sorry not to have it in my power of making them any presents. I only supplied them with some rum, with which they seemed satisfied, and went off assuring me of their peaceful intentions and promising to come down soon with some of their principal chiefs."

The church, which is so hallowing a feature

in the sketch of the Island Town, is suggestive of the persevering devotion of the Catholic Faith to the spiritual welfare of her children. In 1559, when de Luna raised his national flag upon the shores of Santa Maria, his spiritual mother raised her cross beside it. With that sacred symbol she followed him in his explorations through the limitless wilderness, beginning and ending each day with her holy rites. She returned with Arriola, and, as he built his fort, her children under her pious promptings built her church. As the drum beat the reveille to call the soldier to the activities of life, the notes of her bell reminded him of her presence to admonish and console him. The engraving presents the next effort of her zeal. Afterwards, when the wing of the hurricane and the wild fury of the waves had swept away her island sanctuary, and left her children houseless on a desolate shore, she followed them to that hamlet which has just been described, where, around a rude altar, sheltered by the frail thatch of the palmetto, they enjoyed her consoling offices. When, in 1763, their national flag fell from the staff and her people went into voluntary exile, her cross went with them as their guide and solace. She returned with Galvez, and never for a day since then has she been without her altar and her priest on these shores to perform her rites for the living and the dead. For many years after the establishment of American rule, that altar and that priest were the only means by which the Protestant mother, more obedient to the Divine word than sectarian prejudice, could obey the sacred mandate: "Suffer the little children to come unto Me, and forbid them not."

CHAPTER VII.

British West Florida—Pensacola the Capital—Government Established—Johnstone first Governor—British Settlers—First Survey of the Town—Star Fort—Public Buildings—Resignation of Johnstone—His Successor, Monteforte Brown.

THE little settlement, mentioned in the last chapter, soon attained an importance in striking contrast with its appearance and condition.

By the treaty of Paris, France had ceded to Great Britain Canada, and that part of Louisiana east of a line beginning at the source of the Mississippi river and running through its centre to the Iberville river, thence through the middle of this river, lakes Maurepas and Pontchartrain, to the Gulf. That acquisition, with Florida, extended the British North American empire from the Gulf of Mexico to the Arctic Sea, bringing alike the Seminoles and Esquimaux under its dominion.

On the seventh of October, 1763, by a royal

proclamation the limits of the governments of East and West Florida were established; the former extending from the Apalachicola river eastward; the latter embracing all the territory lately acquired from France and Spain south of the parallel of 31° from the Mississippi to the Chattahoochee river; and by another exercise of royal authority, in February, 1764, the northern boundary was pushed to 32°, 28'. This line was also the southern boundary of the territory of Illinois, and it brought Mobile and Natchez within the limits of West Florida.

Of that province, so extensive and so rich in natural resources, Pensacola became the established capital; a natural result of the high estimate placed by the British upon the advantages of the harbor. When Lord Bute's ministry was assailed in the House of Commons for having procured Florida, by the surrender of Cuba, which Great Britain had conquered in the war ended by the treaty of Paris, the acquisition of the Bay of Pensacola figures as a prominent feature in the ministerial defense.

The first step towards the establishment of civil government in West Florida was taken upon the arrival, in February, 1764, at Pensacola, of Commodore George Johnstone of the Royal Navy, who came as the governor of the province; his first official act being a proclamation announcing his presence, powers, jurisdiction, as well as the laws which were to be in force. There came with him the Twenty-first British regiment as a garrison for the post, and also a number of civilians in search of fortune, or new homes; some as parasites, who are never absent where public money is to be distributed, and others attracted by the charms of the district, under the delusive misrepresentations of which the immigrant is so often the victim.

In November, 1764, Governor Johnstone, under instructions from the British government—which from the first seems to have taken a deep interest in the development of its late acquisitions—published a description of the province for the purpose of attracting settlers. By efforts like this, a tide of immigration soon began to flow into West Florida, which, during the British dominion of nearly twenty years, it is estimated, brought into it a population of 25,000. In this inflow were observable a large number of Africans, imported under official encouragement, to clear the forests and till the fields of the province; the British conscience being, then, still enthralled by the greedy slave-traders of Bristol, Liverpool and London, was patiently awaiting the advent of Clarkson and Wilberforce, to quicken it into resistance to the cruel traffic.

In the early days of Governor Johnstone's administration, Pensacola was surveyed and a plan established. The main street was named George, for King George III., and the second street eastward Charlotte, for Queen Charlotte. The area between those streets as far north as what is now Intendencia street was not surveyed into blocks and lots, but reserved as a public place or park. The lots south of Garden street had an area of 80 feet front and 170 in depth. North of that street they were 192 feet square, known as arpent or Garden lots, and numbered to correspond with those lying south of Garden street, which were, strictly speaking, town lots. In order to furnish each family with a garden spot, each grantee of a town lot was entitled, upon the condition of improvement, to receive a conveyance of an arpent lot of the same number as his town lot.

That plan, which was the work of Elias Durnford, appointed, on the twenty-sixth of July, 1764, civil engineer of the province, is still the plan of the old part of Pensacola, with some changes in what was the English park, or public place; and therefore the plan of the town is, strictly speaking, of English origin.

The park, however, though excluded from private ownership, was not intended to be vacant, but on the contrary, was devoted to public uses. In the centre of it was a star-shaped stockade fort, designed as a place of refuge for the population in case of an Indian attack. Near it were the officers' quarters, barracks, guard house, ordinance store-house and laboratory, two powder magazines, the King's bake-house, cooperage shelter, and government store-house. This park was, therefore, in the early days of Pensacola, the liveliest and busiest part of the town.

The star-shaped fort was, from 1764 until after 1772, the only fortification of the town, as may be inferred from the official report of

Captain Thomas Sowers, engineer, on the fifth of April of the latter year.

The first street pushed through the crescent-shaped swamp, was George street, involving much labor in building a causeway and covering it with earth. It extended to the elevation, then named Gage Hill, in honor of General Gage, of Boston memory, and who, as the commander-in-chief of all the royal forces in the British North American colonies, had much to do with Pensacola in its early days. Upon the highest point of this hill was established a lookout from which the approaches of the town landward and seaward could be observed.

Governor Johnstone, who was a commodore in the royal navy, in the second year of his administration, found himself in jarring relations with the military, resulting from circumstances which, at this distance of time, seem to be trifles, but magnified, when they occurred, into importance by that jealous sensitiveness which appears to exist always between those two arms of the public service. As might be expected, whisperers, busybodies, and parasites, thronging the seat of patronage, ready to catch any stray crumb of official favor, aggravated the conflict, which at last became so bitter and widespread that we find it figuring in the records of the courts-martial of a major, a lieutenant, and even an ensign. Naturally, too, the colonists at length became partisans of the official strife, thereby contributing to bring about a condition of affairs rendering the governor's further continuance in office so uninviting to himself and so unsatisfactory to the people that, in December, 1766, he resigned.

An incident which occurred shortly after his appointment, manifests his impatience of criticism—a weakness which may have been the cause of his troubles in Florida. He and Grant, governor of East Florida, were appointed at the same time by the Bute administration, when Scotch appointees to office were so ill-favored by the English. The announcement were made in the *North Briton* with a sarcastic allusion to them as a brace of Scotchmen. At this Johnstone was so much incensed that he sent to the publishers what was equivalent to a challenge. Moreover, on meeting with a Mr. Brooks, who was connected with the *North Briton*, John-

stone insisted on his stating whether he was the
author of the article. Brooks refusing to answer, Johnstone drew his sword to use on him
when by-standers interfered. Brooks instituted
legal proceedings under which the governor was
bound to keep the peace.

In after years, Johnstone became a member of
Parliament, and attracted much attention by
casting, in the House of Commons, one of the
only two negative votes on the Boston Harbor
Bill, Edmund Burke casting the other. His
course on that memorable occasion secured him
such consideration with the Americans as to
induce the British government to select him as
one of the five commissioners who were sent to
America in 1778, under Lord North's conciliatory bill, intended to concede to the colonies all,
and even more, than they had demanded at the
beginning of the controversy with the Mother
country. But the sequel of his mission proved
his unfitness for the position. Besides venturing to enter into correspondence with Robert
Morris and Francis Dana, he attempted, through
a lady, to bribe General Joseph Reed of Pennsylvania by an offer of £10,000 and the highest

office within the gift of the crown in America in the event his efforts at conciliation proving successful. To that offer Reed made the memorable reply: "I am not worth purchasing, but such as I am the King of Great Britain is not rich enough to do it."

The other commissioners, Mr. Eden, General Clinton, and Lord Carlisle, at least, disavowed all knowledge or connection with Johnstone's course. His conduct became the subject of resolutions passed by Congress, in which it was declared: "That it is incompatible with the honor of Congress to hold any manner of intercourse with the said George Johnstone, especially to negotiate with him upon affairs in which the cause of liberty is interested."

From that reflection he sought to vindicate himself by an ill-tempered address, which was followed by his resignation from the commission.

Though a Scotchman, he seems in this affair to have acted with more of the impulse of a Frenchman, like Genet, than with the cool deliberation characteristic of his race. Though he had been a commodore in the British navy, after his appointment of governor of West Florida his historical designation is "Governor Johnstone."

By virtue of his being lieutenant-governor, Monteforte Brown became Johnstone's successor.

The troops stationed at Pensacola during Governor Johnstone's time were the Thirty-first regiment of infantry and the second battalion of Royal Artillery, under General Taylor. In 1765, these troops suffered from scurvy, as a remedy for which the governor undertook means to provide them with fresh meat, a provision which it would seem a thoughtful and considerate ruler would have employed as a preventive, instead of waiting until disease required it as a remedy.

The scourge, however, proved a blessing in the end, as our ills often do, by turning attention to the necessity of securing regular supplies of vegetable food, the acids of which science had determined to be the preventive of scorbutic affections. This led to the clearing, draining and cultivation of large bodies of the Titi Swamp, a process which, once begun, was continued throughout the period of English rule, until the town was surrounded by smiling gardens, extending westward almost to Bayou Chico, of which this generation has evidence in the absence of forest from the district and its meadow-like appearance, as well as its intersections of choked up ditches and drains.

In October, 1766, there was an exhibition in Pensacola of the cruelty with which the British soldier was treated in the last century For absence without leave, James Baker Mattross of the Royal Artillery received 100 lashes under sentence of a court-martial. Harsh as this sentence may seem, it was mild and humane compared with what was inflicted in other instances at other military posts. Soldiers of the Royal American regiment, stationed at Detroit, were punished for rioting, as follows:* James Wilkins, Derby McCaffny, and Sargeant Deck 1000 lashes each, whilst fortunate Corporal Saums escaped with only 500, but who, even in his luck, was yet five times less lucky than the royal artilleryman at Pensacola. These terrible

---

*Canadian Archives (Haldimand Collection), B. 22, p. 262.

inflictions provoke inquiry as to the dermal texture of the backs of the British soldiery of the eighteenth century.

With the possibility of such suffering before them, we can appreciate the joy with which Richard Harris of the Thirty-first regiment, charged with stealing chickens, and Lewis Crow on trial for selling liquor, who were tried by court-martial at the same time as Mattross, received their respective findings of not guilty.

CHAPTER VIII.

General Bouquet—General Haldimand.

EARLY in 1765 General Henry Bouquet having been assigned to the command of the southern military district of the colonies, of which Pensacola was the headquarters, sailed from Philadelphia in a small schooner for that place. He arrived there in the early spring, and on the following September died.* Of the day and cause of his death nothing seems to be known. Of the fact that his grave was marked by a monument, there is the most conclusive proof.†

Where is that monument? That time and the elements are responsible for its disappearance is improbable. That it is not even a

---
*Kingford's History of Canada, Vol. V., p. 110.

†A statement of the English grey bricks used in the monument exists in the Canadian archives at Ottawa, dated February 1, 1770. Haldimand Papers, K. 15, p. 84.

subject of tradition suggests the painful suspicion that it was willfully destroyed; a suggestion which explains the absence of all memorials of the people who must have died in Pensacola during the nearly twenty years of the British dominion, and removes from their generation the reproach of having had no respect for the memory and ashes of their departed friends and comrades.

An exodus of the English occurred in 1783, as a future page will show, like that of the Spaniards in 1763 already mentioned. The town was filled by a new and strange population, whose needs for building material were urgent, and their reverence for the dead too feeble, perhaps, to resist the temptation of supplying their wants by plundering tombs deserted by their natural guardians.

Nature, too, conspired with man in the work of desecration. The necropolis of the English was at the western extremity of the town, extending southward and embracing a slight bluff on the Bay. From 1860 to 1870 the water abraded that place, washing out human bones,

and thus compelled the earth to surrender its
'dead to the sport of the waves.

General Bouquet was born at Rolle, in the
canton of Berne, Switzerland. That he attained
so high a rank is evidence of his merit. His
masterly campaign, in 1763, against the Ohio
Indians, including the Delawares, the Shawnees,
and Mingoes, as related by the classic pen of Dr.
Kingsford, in his History of Canada,* is a most
interesting and striking chapter of our colonial
annals. The result was the removal of a terrible scourge from the western borders of Pennsylvania and Virginia, and the restoration to
liberty and to friends of three hundred white
men and women by a treaty, the terms of
which were left to the discretion of General
Bouquet by General Gage. So highly appreciated were his skill and courage at the time that
both colonies honored him with votes of thanks
for his "great services," which were supplemented by a complimentary letter from the
king.

But the royal letter and his promotion were

---

*Volume V., pp. 93-113.

only Dead Sea apples. Their result was a voyage in a small vessel to the distant shores of the Gulf of Mexico, where he was to die in a few months in a little garrison town with his laurels yet fresh on his brow, away from the friends and that admiring social circle he had left so recently at Philadelphia. Had he been the son, or cousin, whether first, second or third, would have mattered not, of a minister, he would have won a pension and obtained an enviable appointment.

General Bouquet was not only a distinguished soldier, but he also left behind him another claim to distinction in the thirty volumes of manuscript in the British museum, known as the "Bouquet Collection," which now calendared is available to the historical student.

His monument has perished; his bones, perhaps, have been the sport of the unpitying waves; generations have unconsciously trampled on his dust; but, in "the Pantheon of history," his name and his fame are as fresh as when on these shores he drew his last breath and heaved his last sigh.

A letter* from his confidential friend Ourry inspires the suspicion that a romantic passion, nourished by exile and inaction, contributed to his early death. He was devoted to a Miss Willing of Philadelphia, and supposed to be her affianced. A Mr. Francis, a wealthy Londoner, wooed and won the lady whilst the soldier was winning laurels on the western frontier. But for vandal hands his tomb would be a shrine where disappointed love could make its votive offerings.

General Frederick Haldimand was the successor of General Bouquet in the command of the southern district. He, too, was a Swiss, and a native of the Canton of Berne. He had

---

*J'ai lu mon cher ami, et relu avec attention votre triste lettre du premier, et suis sensiblement touché de votre état. Je vois que votre esprit agité, comme la mer après une rude secousse de tremblement de terre, n'a pas encore repris son assiette. Je n'avois que trop bien prévu l'effet funeste; plût à Dieu que je l'eusse aussi bien pu prevenir! . . . Je suis attendri du recit tonchant que vous me faites de votre situation douloureuse, et je vous conjure par ce que vous tenez du plus cher et de plus sacré, de ne vous pas laisser aller à la merci d'une passion qui vous mene, et qui vous privera bientôt, si vous n'y prenez garde, des moyens qui vous restent encore pour la dompter (Kingsford Hist. of Can., Vol. V., p. 110).

held important commands in Canada before he came to Florida. In 1773 he was appointed governor of New York. In the same year, during General Gage's absence in England, he was commander-in-chief of the colonies. He was, from 1778 to 1784, governor-general of Canada. To the qualities of a distinguished soldier, he added ability for civil affairs and the statesmanlike qualities which great crises sometimes require in a military commander, as appears from Lord Dartmouth's correspondence with him during Gage's absence.*

There is an interesting coincidence in the lives of Bouquet and Haldimand. Drawn to each other, doubtless, by the tie of nativity and pro-

---

* I trust the designs of those who have apparently from self-interested motives endeavored to spread an alarm, and create fresh disturbances in consequence of the importation of tea by the East India company will prove abortive. . . . In the present state of uncertainty with regard to what may be the issue of this disagreeable business, I cannot say more to you; and, indeed, the sentiments you have expressed in your former dispatches in respect to the propriety or impropriety of employing a military force in case of civil commotion are so just, and your conduct in that delicate situation so temperate and prudent, as to render any particular instructions from me on that head unnecessary. Dartmouth to Haldimand—Canadian Archives, Series B., Vol. 35, p. 64.

fession, similarity of disposition, interests and fortunes, a life-long friendship was the natural consequence. They were associates in land investments. Bouquet bequeathed his entire estate to his native brother-in-arms, including the valuable collection before referred to. More fortunate than the former, the latter lived to be made a Knight of the Bath, and to die in his native town of Yverdun.*

---

*Kingsford's Hist. of Can., Vol. 4, p. 318.

CHAPTER IX.

Governor Elliott—Social and Military Life in Pensacola—Gentlemen—Women—Fiddles—George Street—King's Wharf on November 14, 1768.

THERE exists evidence in the Canadian archives that, in July, 1767, Mr. Elliot was appointed to succeed Governor Johnstone, but careful search has failed to discover any official act upon which to rest the conclusion that he ever came to the province.

In a note dated eighteenth of October, 1768, at Pensacola, General Haldimand tells Governor Brown that "assistance will be given to land Governor Elliot's baggage, and put the garden in order," in answer, evidently, to a request of Governor Brown, made in expectation of the new governor's early arrival. But these preparations were manifestly made in vain, for in a letter written at Pensacola, in January, 1769, by the general to Mr. John Bradley of

New Orleans, he says: "I hope that these matters will be settled on the arrival of Governor Elliot, daily expected." And numerous papers in the Canadian archives, as well as documents in the American state papers, show that from the eighteenth of December, 1766, up to the appointment of Governor Peter Chester, in 1772, Brown was the acting governor of the province. The evidence is therefore conclusive that though Elliot was appointed, he either died or resigned without ever having gone to the province.

The coming of officers and others from the military posts of the province to headquarters, as well as the frequent courts-martial held there, especially numerous and exciting in 1766-7, enlivened military life at Pensacola.

Of the social life of the town during Johnstone's and Brown's administrations, we have but little information. If, however, the opinion of an official high in rank is to be accepted as evidence, gentlemen were not numerous up to 1767, as will be seen from an extract from a letter of his to a friend: "A ship lately arrived from London, has brought over the chief justice and the attorney-general of the province, and

other gentlemen, who are very much wanted."
But who are and who are not gentlemen? Let the moralist, the sectarian, partisan, votary of sport or fashion, dude, friend, enemy, the prejudiced, the just, the harsh, and the charitable successively sit in judgment upon the same man; what a very chameleon in character will he not appear, as he is reviewed by each of his judges? Of this variety of judgments, an occurrence, at Pensacola during this period, is illustrative.

Major Farmer of the Thirty-fourth regiment of infantry, stationed at Fort Charlotte,* was by the Johnstone party accused of embezzlement and fraud. But a court-martial which sat at Pensacola honorably acquitted him, and upon a review of the record the finding of the court was approved by the King.

Another letter, in 1770, gives the following uninviting picture of the civil as well as the social condition of the place: "Pensacola has been justly famed for vexatious law-suits. It is contrived, indeed, that if a poor man owes but five pounds, and has not got so much ready money,

---

* Formerly Fort Condé at Mobile.

or if he disputes some dollars of imposition that may be in the account, or if he is guilty of shaking his fist at any rascal that has abused him, he is sure to be prosecuted, and the costs of every suit are about seven pounds sterling. . . . I have known this province for a little more than four years, yet I could name to you a set of men who may brag of one governor resigned, one horse-whipped and one whom they led by the nose and supported while it suited their purpose, and then betrayed him. What the next turn of affairs will be, God knows."

Perhaps, however, the writer owed a shopkeeper who sued him; or he had been fined for offering violence to some other importunate creditor; and as to the costs of litigation, it is likely, that in this year of grace some luckless litigant, in the modern Pensacola, can be found who would heave a sympathetic sigh on reading the complaint which comes to us from a suitor in its early days.

Besides, the reference to the treatment received by three governors, in a letter written in 1770, is rather puzzling, for though three governors had been appointed for West Florida up to that time, but two, Johnstone and Brown, administered its government. Johnstone resigned and, therefore, Brown must have been the man, if any, who was horsewhipped and led by the nose. As "led by the nose," however, is a metaphor, "horsewhipped" may, perhaps, be regarded as a figure of speech likewise.

Strange though it be, yet so it is, in the mass of Pensacola correspondence, from 1763 to 1770, we find mention made of military officers of every grade, governors, secretaries, surveyors, judges, male Indians, ships, boats, bricks, lumber, shingles, wine, swords, muskets, cheese, cannon and fiddles, but of a woman or any of her belongings, never, with only two exceptions.

One comes to us like an attractive mirage on the far-off horizon of this Sahara of masculinity and soulless things in the person of Mrs. Hugh Wallace of Philadelphia, a friend of General Haldimand, in respect to whom, in a letter to her husband, he says: "I beg my best respects may be acceptable to Mrs. Wallace." The other is a nameless moral wreck, of whom the writer of a letter exclaims: "I wish I could make the mother of my children my wife!" forcing upon the imagination the shadow of a wronged wife, with one's heart touched by the probable sorrows of a blighted life.

But, though excluded from men's letters, we do not need their correspondence to inform us that wives, mothers, sisters and nurses formed no inconsiderable part of the population of Pensacola in those early days, for we know it as certainly, fully, and confidently as we know the town must have been blessed with air, light, food, and all the other vivifying conditions of human existence.

It has been intimated that fiddles were the subject of correspondence, and thuswise. It appears that General Haldimand was the owner of two fiddles. Whether fiddling was one of his accomplishments does not appear. But as ownership of one fiddle ordinarily creates the presumption that the owner is a performer in some one of the three degrees of good, bad or indifferent, the ownership of two would seem to be conclusive of the fact.

However that may be, it seems that Governor Thomas Penn of Pennsylvania had knowledge of the instruments, and, presumably, knowing their merits, coveted them to such a degree that the general induced him to pay $360 for them. As the bargain was made by letter, after the general and the fiddles had been in Pensacola for several years, we may infer that their dulcet tones must have made a deep and ineffaceable impression upon the governor, which no other fiddles could remove. By a vessel sailing from Pensacola to Philadelphia, the general sent a box containing the two fiddles to Mr. Joseph Shipping of that place, agent of Governor Penn, and also a letter to Hugh Ross, his own agent, whom he tells (evidently with the chuckle of a trader who has made a good bargain) of the $360 he is to collect from Shipping, closing the letter with the exclamation, "I wish I had more fiddles to sell!"

Correspondence in 1767 shows courtesies exchanged between Pensacola and Philadelphia. A Pensacolian sends a sea turtle, and the Philadelphian returns a cheese.

The town was accused of being hot and inhospitable. But the letter of complaint tells what a specific wine is for the prevention of all climatic diseases and the other ills of life. One gentleman, to be sure of a supply of the panacea, orders a pipe of old Madeira.

On November 14, 1768, we are walking down the east side of George street from the gardens to the Bay. After passing two blocks we find ourselves on the Public Square and in front of a large building. Going in and out of that building are many people, the most of them soldiers and Indians, and somewhere in or about it we find a Mr. Arthur Neil. Upon inquiry we are informed the building is the king's store-house, and Mr. Neil its keeper. Leaving the store, a short walk brings us to the shore and afterwards to the king's wharf, which we see covered with troops, some of them getting into boats, whilst others, already embarked, are going to a ship lying at anchor. That ship is the *Pensacola* bound for Charleston, South Carolina. The troops are the Thirty-first regiment, lately stationed at Mobile, whence they have just arrived, after an overland march, for the purpose of embarking in the *Pensacola*. Whether they shall remain at Charleston in winter quarters will, according to a letter of General Haldimand to Colonel Chisolm, "depend upon the conduct of the Bostonians."*

---

* Can. Archives, B. 14, pp. 31, 37, 41.

CHAPTER X.

Governor Peter Chester—Fort George of the British and St. Michael of the Spanish—Tartar Point—Red Cliff.

PETER CHESTER, having been commissioned governor of West Florida in 1772, came to Pensacola, the capital of the province, and entered upon the administration of the office. He was recognized and deferred to by General Haldimand as a man of capacity and experience, a reputation which was not impaired by his nine years' rule in Florida.

The first days of his administration were marked by a determination to reform the public service, and to supersede the old star fort by more stable and efficient defenses for the town and harbor, and the spirit which animated him was at once communicated to the military commander of the province.

Early in his administration, after much discussion by engineers of several plans for the defense of the town, a fort was built, under orders from General Gage, on Gage Hill, and named Fort George for his majesty George III.*

In the centre of the fortress was the council chamber of the province and the repository of its archives, where the office duties of the governor and the military commander were performed, where audience was given to Indian chiefs and delegations, and where really centered the government of West Florida, according to its English boundaries.

In that chamber on one occasion could have been seen a man in the prime of life, partly in Indian dress, in earnest conversation with Governor Chester and William Panton, the millionaire and merchant prince of the Floridas. By the evident admixture of white and Indian blood in his veins, his skin had lost several shades of the hue, his hair the peculiar stiffness, and his cheek bones somewhat of the prominence of those of his aboriginal ancestry. He was tall and slender; his eyes, black and piercing, beamed

---

* Mr. Fairbanks, in his 'History of Florida,' calls the fort St. Michael; but that was, in fact, a name bestowed upon it after 1783, when Florida became a Spanish colony.

with the light that belongs to those of the cultured; the Indians said his high forehead was arched like a horse-shoe; the fingers which hold the pen with which he is writing, during a pause in the conversation, are long and slender; he speaks and then reads what he has written; all is in the purest English, to which he is capable of giving point by an apt classical quotation. On a future occasion he will enter that chamber with the commission of a British colonel. A few years later he will hold a like commission from the King of Spain. A few years later still will find him a brigadier-general of the United States. That man is Alexander McGillivray, of whom much is to be written.

In that chamber three men were once seated at a table, attended by two secretaries busily writing, one in English, the other in Spanish. One of the three is Governor Chester, another is General John Campbell, a distinguished English officer whom fortune has just deserted. The third, a young-looking Spaniard, too young for his insignia of a Spanish general, is Don Bernardo de Galvez, the governor and military commander of Louisiana. Those three men are closing a drama and writing the last paragraph of a chapter of history. The two papers the secretaries are writing, when signed, will separate, one going to London, the other to Madrid, to meet again at Versailles. At Versailles they will be copied substantially into the duplicates of the treaty of 1783 between Spain and Great Britain, and constitute its V Article.

A pigeon-hole on the side of that chamber once contained an order from Lord Dartmouth, dated January, 1774, to the commander-in-chief of West Florida, to forward a regiment from Pensacola to revolutionary Boston to quell the tea-riots. This book is debtor to many documents which once rested in other pigeon-holes of the chamber.

Fort George was a quadrangle with bastions at each corner. There were within the fort a powder magazine and barracks for the garrison, besides the chamber above mentioned. The woods north of it, for an' eighth of a mile, and within a curve bending around it to the bay, were felled, in order to give play to its guns landward, whilst they could bear upon an enemy in the bay by firing over the town. By a system of signals, intercommunication was kept up with Tartar Point and thence with Red Cliff.

Tartar Point, now the site of the Navy Yard, where a battery and barracks were erected by the British, is the only existing name in this part of West Florida which carries one's thoughts back to the days of British rule. The name of the point under the second Spanish dominion, which lasted about forty years, was *Punta de la Asta Bandera*—the Point of the Flagstaff. It seems strange that an English name which had been superseded for that period by a Spanish designation, should after that lapse of time be restored.

The locality of Red Cliff was for a time a puzzle. Such a name for a locality at once induced a search for a suggestive aspect. No red bluff, however, not too far eastward to serve as the site of a work for the defense of the town or harbor, could be found, and yet, no bluff westward of the former could be observed to suit the designation. But at length, a letter in the Canadian archives fixed Barrancas as the locality by stating that there was at about the distance of a half to a quarter of a mile from Red

Cliff a powder magazine, built by the Spaniards, capable of holding 500 barrels of powder, which was then being used as the powder depôt of the province, evidently the relic of old San Carlos, destroyed by the French in 1719, and stood on the site of the present Fort Redoubt.

The defenses of Red Cliff consisted of two batteries, "one on the top and the other at the foot of the hill." There were quarters for the officers and barracks for the soldiers in one building, so constructed as to be proof against musket balls and available as an ample defense against an Indian attack.*

---

* Canadian Archives—Rept. of T. Sowers, Capt. Engineers Series B., Vol. XVII., page 302.

CHAPTER XI.

Representative Government.

WHEN the governments of West and East Florida were established, as before related, their governors were, severally, vested with authority, their councils consenting and the condition of the provinces being favorable, to call for the election of general assemblies by the people.

In 1773, Governor Chester concluded that the time had arrived when it would be expedient for him to exercise this power. He, accordingly, issued writs authorizing an election, fixing the time it was to be held, the voting precincts, the qualifications of voters, and the number and qualifications of assemblymen to be chosen, as well as the day of the sitting of the general assembly at Pensacola.

But the writs, unhappily, fixed the terms of assemblymen at **three** years; a provision which proved fatal, not only to this first attempt, but likewise to all future efforts to establish representative government in West Florida. The election was held throughout the province, and the members of a full general assembly elected. But whilst the people went to the polls with alacrity, and hailed with pleasure the advent of popular government, they were opposed to the long tenure fixed by Governor Chester; and so determined was that opposition that they resolved that it should not receive the implied sanction of their votes. They accordingly cast ballots which declared that they were subject to the condition that the representative should hold for one year only. To that condition the governor refused to consent. The people, on the other hand, were equally unyielding in their opposition. Efforts were made, but in vain, to induce a concession by one side or the other; consequently, during the following years of English dominion, as before, the province knew no other civil government than that of the governor and his council.

It is difficult to understand the motives which prompted the people to so stubborn an opposition. The tenure of three years might, indeed, seem long to voters who had probably lived in colonies, where it was a third or two-thirds less. But still, if there was any value to a people in representative government, surely an assembly holding for three years was better than none; especially as it would have so concentrated the influence and power of the community as to enable it at some auspicious conjuncture to remove the one popular objection to the system.

On the other hand, we can better appreciate the conduct of Governor Chester. An Englishman with the Tory conservatism of that day, he would, naturally, fear the effect of short terms and frequent elections, aside from economical considerations. All the northern colonies were in a state of ferment bordering on revolution, and that consideration, doubtless, intensified his opposition to anything that savored of opposition to the wishes of the king or his representatives. Indeed, from his stand-point, to yield to the popular wishes in array against his own will and judgment, was to leaven the province with a pestilent political heresy which was seeking to substitute the power of the people for the authority of the crown.

Governor **Chester** seems to have possessed superior talents for government, the best evidence of which is found in the prosperity of the colony during his administration, the harmony that existed between him and the military, and the high respect and deference he received from General **Haldimand.**

Such a man, conscious of his rectitude and good intentions towards the province, evinced by his readiness to afford it the privilege of representative government, somewhat at the expense of his own authority, would naturally feel that the condition attached to the ballots, and adhered to with much insistance, manifested such a want of confidence in him as to justify his distrust of the people.

But what Governor Chester's zealous endeavors could not accomplish in West Florida, the reluctant efforts of Governor Tonyn achieved in the eastern province. In 1780, the latter, against his own wishes, and solely at the suggestion of others, called for the election of a general assembly. The call having been promptly obeyed, the first popular representative body in Florida met at St. Augustine in January, 1781.*

---

*Fairbank's **Florida,** p. 232.

CHAPTER XII.

Growth of Pensacola—**Panton,** Leslie & Co.—A King and the Beaver—**Governor** Chester's Palace and Chariot—The White House of the British, and Casa Blanca of the Spanish—General Gage—Commerce—Earthquake.

THERE is evidence of great improvement in the town within a few years from Governor Chester's advent; a progress which was accelerated as the revolution in the Northern Colonies advanced. That great movement, ever widening its area, extended at last from the Gulf to Canada, leaving no repose or peace for those who, living within it, were resolute to remain loyal to their king.

Some entered the royal military service; multitudes left America, and others, to nurse their loyalty in quietude, removed to Florida. Though most of that emigration went to East Florida, yet West Florida, and especially Pensacola, received a large share. St. Augustine, however, was the tory paradise of the revolutionary era. She can, without question, supplement the glory of her antiquity with the boast of having once seen her streets lighted up by the blazing effigies of John Adams and John Hancock.*

The most important commercial acquisition of Pensacola by that tory immigration was William Panton, the senior of the firm of Panton, Leslie & Co., a Scotch house of great wealth and extensive commercial relations. They had an establishment in London, with branches in the West India Islands. During the English dominion in Florida they established themselves in St. Augustine; later, during Governor Chester's administration, at Pensacola, and afterwards, at Mobile. Other merchants also came to Pensacola about the same time, attracted principally by the heavy disbursements of the government. But these expenditures were not the attraction to the Scotchmen. Their object was to grasp the Indian trade of West Florida. A building which they erected

---

*Fairbank's History of Florida, p. 223.

with a wharf in front of it is still standing, or at least, its solid brick walls are now those of the hospital of Dr. James Herron, whose dwelling house stands on the site of the Council Chamber of Fort George.

In that building was carried on a business which grew steadily from year to year during the British dominion, and afterwards attained great magnitude under Spanish rule, as we shall have occasion to notice in a future page. In building up that business, Panton had a most able and influential coadjutor in General Alexander McGillivray, whom we lately saw in the Council Chamber of Fort George. Through him their business comprehended not only West Florida, but extended to and even beyond the Tennessee river. In perfect security, their long lines of pack horses went to and fro in that great stretch of country, carrying all the supplies the Indians needed, and bringing back skins, peltry, bees-wax, honey, dried venison, and whatever else their savage customers would provide for barter. Furs were a large item of that traffic, for the beaver in those days abounded throughout West Florida, and was found even in the vicinity of Pensacola.

One of their ponds, still existing on Carpenter's Creek, four miles from the town, is suggestive of an instructive comparison between the fruits of the life-work of its humble constructors, and those of the twenty years rule, of a mighty monarch. Of the British dominion of his Majesty George III, in this part of Florida, the millions of treasure expended, and the thousands of lives sacrificed to establish and maintain it, there exists no memorial, or result, except a fast disappearing bank of sand on the site of Fort George. From that barren outcome of such a vast expenditure of human life and money, we turn with a blush for the vanity and folly of man, to contemplate that little pool fringed with fairy candles,* where the water lilies bloom, and the trout and perch flash in the sunlight, as the memento of a perished race,

---

* A name which the children of the neighborhood have bestowed on the bloom of a water plant, suggested by its wax like stem and its yellow point, and here mentioned to suggest to our people that it is time we should have popular designations for others of our beautiful wild flowers.

whose humble labors have furnished pastime and food to successive generations of anglers.

An unsuccessful effort has been made to obtain reliable information as to the number and description of the houses Pensacola contained in its most thriving days during Governor Chester's administration. But the only account we have, is that of William Bertram, who though reputed an eminent botanist is hardly reliable, for he describes Governor Chester's residence as a "stone palace, with a cupola built by the Spaniards;"* and yet, according to the description of the town in Captain Will's report, at the close of Spanish rule, it consisted of "forty huts and barracks, surrounded by a stockade;" and he witnessed at that time, the exodus of the entire Spanish population. Besides, persons whose memories went back within thirty years of Governor Chester's alleged palatial residence, neither saw, nor even heard, of the ruins of such a structure.

Upon the same authority rests the statement, that the Governor had a farm to which he took

---

* Fairbanks Florida, p. 219.

morning rides in "his chariot."* But a traveler whose fancy was equal to the transformation of a hut into a palace, may have transformed his excellency's modest equipage into a more courtly vehicle.

It is probable, however, that although Governor Chester was not the occupant of a stone palace with a cupola, he lived in a sightly and comfortable dwelling built of brick or wood, or perhaps of both. One such dwelling of his time, that of William Panton, was familiar, forty years ago to the elders of this generation. It stood near the business house of Panton, Leslie & Co. Taking its style and solidity as a guide, there existed several houses in the town within the last half century that could be identified as belonging to Governor Chester's day.

One of them was the scene of a tragedy; a husband cutting a wife's throat fatally, his own more cautiously, or perhaps her cervical vertibrae had taken off the edge of the razor, for he survived. Thereafter, none would inhabit it, and consequently it rapidly went to ruin. It

---

*Pickett, Vol. II. p. 25.

stood on the north side of Government street, a block and a half from Palafox. A jury acquitted him. Why? No one could conjecture, unless because she was his wife, and therefore his chattel, like the cow or sheep of a butcher.

In Governor Chester's time there existed a large double story suburban residence, which was a distinguished feature in the landscape looking southwesterly from Fort George, or from any part of the Bay. It stood on the bluff between the now Perdido R. R. and Bayou Chico. Painted white, it became the "white house" of the English, and "Casa Blanca" of the Spanish dominion.

It was the home of a family of wealth and social standing, composed of three—husband, wife, and daughter, the latter a child. Gardens belonging to it covered much of the area of that meadow-like district already mentioned. That home was to be the scene of a drama in three acts; the death of a child, the death of a husband, and a struggle of strong, martyrlike womanhood in the toils of temptation, tried to the lowest depth of her being, but coming forth triumphant.

In examining the calendar of the Haldimand collection by Mr. Douglas Brymner, Archivest of the Dominion of Canada, we are impressed with the great and varied responsibility, labor, and care, attending the office of commander in chief of the American colonies, especially after Great Britain's, Canada, Florida, and Louisiana acquisitions. His administration involved not merely general superintendence of the military department, but likewise embraced the minutest details requiring expenditures of public money. We accordingly find General Gage, during Governor Chester's administration, dictating letters in respect to carpenter's wages* in Pensacola. Again we find him busy over a controversy which had sprung up there in respect to the employment of a Frenchman, Pierre Rochon, † to do carpenter's work, and furnish shingles, to the exclusion of Englishmen. Upon economical grounds his excellency decided in favor of Rochon. Pierre was evidently an active and enterprising man. Before he came to Pensacola

---

* Canadian Archives B. Vol. 15, p. 267.
† Id. 15 p. 195.

to secure for himself all the public carpentering and shingle business there, he had enjoyed the like monopoly at Mobile.

Again we find the General engaged with a small matter at Red Cliff.* Lieutenant Cambell, of the engineer department, had furnished some carpenters who were employed there with candles and firewood, doubtless because they could not otherwise be procured by the men. That act of kindness brought the benevolent lieutenant the following scorching reproof: "I am sorry to acquaint you that his excellency, General Gage, is greatly displeased at your giving of the carpenters candles and firewood; and he desires to know by what authority you assumed to give those allowances, or by what order they were given? For his excellency declares, that a shilling shall not be paid on that account." New York, 16 Feb. 1773. S. Sowers, Captain of Engineers.

Even the quality of bricks used on the public works at Pensacola was a matter of interest to the commander in chief. In 1771, a brick man-

---

*Id. 17 p. 267.

ufactured by the British, and one by the Spaniards, nearly a century before, as General **Haldimand** says, were sent to headquarters at New York, for the judgment of his excellency as to their comparative merits.

These letters impress us the more with the cares of General Gage, when we reflect they were written at the time of the troublesome tea business at rebellious Boston; and when the flowing tide of the revolution, as may be discerned from almost every page of the calendar, was daily rising, and threatening to sweep away the supports of British authority in the colonies.

In a former page mention is made of a Philadelphia lady, whose name occurs in the Pensacola correspondence of an earlier day. It is but fair, therefore, that we should not leave unnoticed a New York lady who is mentioned in letters of Governor Chester's time; the more so, because she seems to have been one of those thrifty housewives, who do not entirely depend upon the tin can, and green glass jar of the shop to supply their families with preserved fruits and vegetables; besides, there can be brought in with her extracts from letters, exemplary of the courtly style, with which in Governor Chester's day, a gentleman returned, and a lady received his thanks for a small courtesy.*

General **Haldimand**, at Penascloa, writes Captain S. Sowers, the husband of the lady, who is in New York:

"I most respectfully ask Mrs. Sowers, to permit me, through you, to tender to her my most grateful thanks for the three jars of pickels."

The Captain replies: "Mrs. Sowers, with pleasure, accepts your thanks for the pickels, and when ye season comes for curing of them, she will send you another collection which she hopes will be acceptable."

In this stirring, short-hand, type-writing age, the form of a like exchange of courtesies would probably be: "Pickels received. Thanks."

Though there was no lack of lawyers and doctors, who it is said, lived in fine style, there was a sad want of clergymen or preachers in the province. There was but one of whom we have any account up to 1779, and he was stationed at Mobile. **Stuernagel**, the Waldeck Field

---

*Canadian Archives B. Vol. 15 p. 161.

Preacher, on his arrival in Pensacola, in that year, christened a boy whose parents had been waiting eight years to make him the subject of the holy office. He also baptized men who had been watching from their boyhood for an opportunity to make their baptismal vows. Nor can there be found a reference to church or chapel during the English dominion.*

The most prosperous and promising days Pensacola ever saw, except those since the close of the civil war, were from 1772 to 1781. As the American revolution advanced, additions were made to the numbers, intelligence and wealth of its population, owing to causes already mentioned. It was the capital of a province rich in its forests, its agricultural and other resources. Its Bay was prized as the peerless harbor of the Gulf, which it was proposed by the British government to make a great naval station, a beginning in that direction having been made by selecting a site for a navy yard adjoining the town to the westward. Its commerce was daily on the increase; not only in consequence

---

* Von Elking Vol. 11 p. 139.

of the extension of Panton, Leslie & Co.'s trade with the Indians, but other enterprising merchants who had been added to the population, were engaged in an export trade, comprising pine timber and lumber, cedar, salt beef, raw hides, cattle, tallow, pitch, bear's oil, staves, shingles, honey, beeswax, salt fish, myrtle wax* deer skins, dried venison, furs and peltry. This trade, and the £200,000 annually extended by the British government, as well as the disbursements of the shipping, constituted the sources of the prosperity of the town.

This period, besides being a season of growth and prosperity to Pensacola, as well as the rest of the Province, was one of repose, undisturbed by the march of armies, battles, and the other cruel shocks of war that afflicted the northern colonies. But it was not to remain to the end a quiet spectator of the drama enacting on the continent. It, too, had an appointment with fate. Though not even a faint flash of the northern storm was seen on its horizon, yet

---

* This is the product of the wild myrtle, obtained by putting the seed into hot water, when the wax liquifies and floats on the surface.

there had been one for long brooding for it in the southwest.

The earthquake, too, that visited it on the night of February 6, 1780,* was but a presage of that which on May 8, 1781, was to shake it to its center; and prove the signal of an exodus of the English almost as complete as was that of the Spanish population in 1763.

---

*On the sixth of Febuary 1780, at night, a fearful storm arose with repeated thunder and lightning. An earthquake was accompanied by such a violent shock, that in the barracks the regimentals and the arm racks fell from the walls in a great many places, and everything was moved in the rooms. The doors were sprung, chimneys were thrown together, and from the fires burning on the hearths, a conflagration threatened to burst forth. Neighboring houses clashed together, and those buried in the ruins cried for help. The sea foamed and raged; the thunder continually rolled. It was a terrible night. Only towards one o'clock, the raging elements in some measure again became subdued. Wonderful to relate, no human life was lost."—Von Elking, Vol. 11, p. 144.

CHAPTER XIII.

Military Condition of West Florida in 1778—General John Campbell—The Waldecks—Spain at War with Britain—Bute, Baton Rouge and Fort Charlotte Capitulate to Galvez—French Town—Famine in Fort George—Galvez's Expedition against Pensacola—Solana's Fleet Enters the Harbor—Spaniards Effect a Landing—Spanish Entrenchment Surprised—The Fall of Charleston Celebrated in Fort George.

THE military condition of West Florida was changed as the revolutionary war progressed There were no longer seen two or more regiments at Pensacola, one or two at Mobile, and one at Fort Bute, Baton Rouge, and Panmure. The call for troops for service in the northern colonies had, by the latter part of 1778, reduced the entire effective force of the province to five hundred men.

That such a reduction was thought prudent, was due to the peaceful relations of the Spaniards and the British, as well as those of the latter with the Creek and Choctaw Indians, attributable to the influence of McGillivray, now a colonel in the British service.

In the latter part of 1778, however, the British government becoming suspicious of Spain, and anticipating her alliance with France, ordered General Clinton to reinforce West Florida. Accordingly, General John Campbell, a distinguished officer, was sent to Pensacola, with a force of 1,200 men, composed of a regiment of Waldecks, and parts of two regiments of Provincials from Maryland and Pennsylvania. They did not arrive, however, until the twenty-ninth of January, 1779.*

---

*It is to the presence of these Waldecks at the siege and capture of Pensacola, that we are indebted for the only detailed account we possess of those events. The Waldeck regiment was one of the many mercenary bodies of German troops which Great Britain hired to conquer her revolted colonies. On the return of the commands to Germany, after the close of the war, each commander was required to make to his government a detailed report of its experiences. In 1863, Max Von Elking published, at Hanover, two volumes containing the substance of those reports, entitled:

["Die deutchen Hülfstruppen im Nordamerikanischen Befrenings Kriege, 1776 bis 1783."]

The German Troops in the North American War of Independence, 1776 to 1783.

Those of the Waldecks extended from the day the regiment was completed at Corbach, where it was reviewed by the widowed Princess of Waldeck, and her court ladies,

Early in 1789, General Campbell sent two companies of Waldecks to reinforce Fort Bute, which brought its garrison up to about 500 men under the command of Lt. Colonel Dickson.

At length Spain threw off the mask, and adopted a course which justified the suspicions of the British Court as to her inimical intentions. On June 16, the Spanish minister, the Marquis d' Almodovar, having delivered to Lord Weymouth a paper equivalent to a declaration of war, immediately departed from London without taking leave. Spain thereupon became an ally of France, but not of the United States. Nevertheless, under the influence of the Court of Versailles, Don Bernardo de Galvez,

---

on May 9, 1776, up to the return of its small remnant in 1783. The princess entertained them, and furnished them besides 100 guelden for a jollification—doubtless out of the hire she received for the hapless creatures. The remark of a courtier, that he would see "all those who came back riding in carriages," indicates the delusive hopes with which it was sought to inspire them. Nevertheless, it was thought prudent by the Princess, that the departing mercenaries should, to prevent desertion, be guarded during their journey to the Weser, where they were to embark, by the Green Regiment of Sharpshooters. The regiment consisted of 640 men, under the command of Colonel Von Hanuxleden. Stuernagel was the Field Preacher, or chaplain, to whose journey Von Elking makes many references.

the Governor of Louisiana, on June 19, published, at New Orleans, the proclamation of the Spanish King, acknowledging the independence of the United States. The dates of these transactions furnish conclusive evidence of a pre-arrangement, designed to enable the Spaniards to assail the British posts in West Florida before they could be succored by the home government.

In pursuance of that policy, Galvez at once began his preparations for offensive operations against Forts Bute, Baton Rouge and Panmure, in the order in which they are mentioned. The great distance of Pensacola from them, as well as the want of facilities of communication, assured him that with an adequate force at his command, General Campbell's first intimation of his operations would be the news of their capture.

In August, with a force of 2,000 men, Galvez began his advance on Fort Bute. As soon as Dickson was informed of his movement, he resolved to concentrate his forces at Baton Rouge, leaving at the former post a few men to man the guns, and to make such a show of resistance as would give him time to perfect the defenses of the latter.

On August 30, Galvez appeared before Bute. After a contest of some hours, its handful of defenders arrested his movements by the time consumed in an honorable capitulation. Bute having been secured, Galvez pushed on to Baton Rouge. In his first attack, he was repulsed with the heavy loss of 400 men killed and wounded, which was within 100 of Dickson's entire force. In the next attack which was made on the following day, the Spanish loss was 150. Although the loss on his side was in both attacks only 50 men, Dickson realizing that he was cut off from all succor, and that he must either surrender, or see his command gradually waste away under the repeated attacks of an overwhelming enemy, capitulated upon the most honorable terms. The command was pledged not to fight against Spain for eighteen months unless sooner exchanged. With loaded guns and flags flying the garrison was to march to the beat of the drum 500 paces from the fort and there stack arms. The officers were to retain their swords and every one his private property. All were to be cared for and transported to a British harbor by the Spaniards.* Fort Panmure, from which the garrison had been withdrawn for the defense of Baton Rouge, was included in the surrender.

It was not until the twentieth of October that a courier brought to Pensacola intelligence of the fall of the Mississippi Posts, although Baton Rouge had surrendered during the first days of September. When it was received it was not credited, but regarded as a false report coming from the Spaniards to entice the British commander from Pensacola in order that it might be captured in his absence. Even the report of a second courier coming, on the twenty-third, failed at first to work conviction; but at last all doubt was dispelled, and every effort directed to putting Pensacola in a defensive condition.

Why Galvez did not follow up his success at Baton Rouge by an immediate advance on Mobile, it is difficult to conceive, except upon the presumption of his ignorance of the weakness of the military forces there, and at Pensacola.

---

*Von Elking, Vol. 11, p. 142.

In December, 1779, Clinton's expedition against Charleston sailed from New York; its destination veiled in such secrecy, that even General Washington, as well as the rest of the world outside of the British lines, was in the dark respecting it. Miralles, the Spanish agent, feared it was intended to recover the conquests of Galvez in West Florida, and signified so much in a letter to General Washington. By the time the letter was received, however, the General had become convinced "that the Carolinas were the objects," and in reply so tells the Spanish agent.

It was during the interval of Galvez's inaction between the capture of Baton Rouge, and his attack on Mobile, that Chevalier de la Luzerne had a conference with General Washington, on the fifteenth of September, 1789, at West Point, with the view of bringing about such concert of movement in the American forces in the Carolinas and Georgia, and the Spanish forces in Florida, as would be a check on the British in their movements against either.* But with

---

* Sparks, Vol. 6, p. 542.

every disposition for such co-operation, the latter being without authority to that end, went no further than to show his sympathy with the Spaniards, and his readiness to afford advice and information, which he afterwards manifested in the letter to Miralles above mentioned.

In that letter, referring to the capture of Fort Bute and Baton Rouge, he says: "I am happy of the opportunity of congratulating you on the important success of His Majesty's arms." It is hardly probable, however, that General Washington would have been so ready to congratulate Miralles on those successes, had he known that in consequence of Galvez's bad faith, their result would be to increase the ranks of the foe he was fighting.

In the beginning of March, 1780, Galvez again began military operations, by advancing against Fort Charlotte. On the twelfth, after his demand for a surrender had been refused by Captain Durnford, the British commander, the fort was assailed by six batteries.

By the fourteenth, after a conflict of ten days, a practicable breach having been made, Durnford capitulated upon the same terms which

Dickson had exacted at Baton Rouge. Hunger had conspired with arms to make capitulation a necessity. For several days before that event the garrison had been comparatively without food. When the gallant Durnford marched out of the breach at the head of a handful of hunger-smitten men, Galvez is said to have manifested deep mortification at having granted such favorable terms to so feeble a foe. An effort was made by General Campbell to relieve Fort Charlotte, but it fell just as succor was at hand. The delay in rendering it was occasioned by rain storms, which, having flooded the country, greatly impeded the movements of the relieving force. *

The gallant defense of Fort Charlotte by Durnford seems to have lead Galvez to reflections which ended in the conclusion that he was not, then, strong enough to attack Pensacola. He,

---

* Von Elking, Vol. 11, pp. 144–5. "It proved a horrible march. It almost continually rained. The men were forced to wade up to their ankles through the soft ground, or through mud. It was only possible to cross the greatly swollen streams by means of the trunks of the trees. The men could only pass singly on them, and the one who missed his footing, and stept into the water below was irretrievably lost."

accordingly, made no further movement, until he had procured from Havana a supply of heavy artillery, and a large additional force.

That it was a part of his plan to advance upon Pensacola immediately after the capture of Mobile, is evidenced by the Spanish Admiral Solana's fleet appearing, and anchoring off the harbor, on March 27, hovering about as if in expectation of a signal from the land until the thirtieth, and then sailing away. The appearance of a scouting party of Spaniards about the same time, on the east side of the Perdido, likewise pointed to such a design.

Be that as it may, Galvez made no further movement in West Florida until February, 1781, the eventful year of the great American rally; the year that witnessed Morgan's brilliant victory, on the seventeenth of January at the Cowpens; and Green's masterly strategy, culminating on the fifteenth of March at Guildford Court House in an apparent defeat, but in sequence, a victory, for it sent Cornwallis to Yorktown for capture on the nineteenth of October.

As we contemplate that year, big with the fate of empire on this continent, the imagination is captivated by the spectacle of a line of battle extending from the northern limits of Maine to the mouth of the Mississippi; the intense points of action being Cowpens, Guildford Court House, Pensacola and Yorktown.

That no reinforcement was sent to General Campbell, although the fall of Fort Charlotte was a warning that Galvez's next effort would be against Pensacola, manifests the strain which Britain's contest with her colonies and France had brought upon both her naval and military resources. When, therefore, in February, 1781, Galvez was about to advance against the place with a large fleet and an army of 15,000 men, according to the lowest estimate, the British force numbered about 1,000* regular troops, besides some provincials.

The British looked for some aid from the Creek, Choctaw and Chickasaw Indians. It was a body of the latter which drove the Spanish scouts across the Perdido shortly after the capture of Mobile.

The three tribes were loyal to their white

---

*Von Elking, Vol. II., p. 152.

allies, even when the latter were no longer able to furnish them with their customary supplies. The Spaniards, on the other hand, with everything to offer them, utterly failed to shake their British loyalty. As illustrative of their devotion, it is related when the Waldecks landed at Pensacola, the Indians, inferring from their strange language that they were enemies, inclined to attack them. They had the prudence, however, to call upon Governor Chester for an explanation. After he had satisfactorily answered the question "whether the men of strange speech were the friends or foes of their Great White Brother on the other side of the big water," they manifested great joy and honored the strangers with a salute from their rifles.

When, however, the advance on Pensacola by the Spaniards was abandoned in the spring of 1780, and thence up to the following December General Campbell found his savage allies rather an encumbrance than a benefit. That time was devoted to strengthening Fort George and the defenses of the harbor, a labor in which no reward could induce them to assist. The exciting occupation of taking Spanish scalps, for which £3* were paid, however, was one in which they could render a barbarous service to the British.

The Indians were under the command of a Marylander, formerly an ensign in the British army, who, whilst stationed at Pensacola, had been cashiered for misconduct. He afterwards went to the Creek Nation, where he married the daughter of a chief. Though vainly styling himself General William Augustus Bowles, he was content to accept restoration to his rank of ensign as a reward for the service, which, at the head of his band of Creeks, Choctaws and Chickasaws, he was expected to render to the British during Galvez's operations in West Florida.

In the latter months of 1780, Pensacola and the garrison of Fort George were on the point of starvation. All the resources of the British government seem to have been required for the great struggle of 1781 on the Atlantic coast, and Galvez's conquest had cut off the customary

---

* Von Elking, Vol. II., p. 140.

supplies from the rich country lying between Mobile Bay and the Mississippi.

Field-preacher Stuernagel says in his journal: "This morning we drank water and ate a piece of bread with it. At mid-day we had just nothing to drink but water. Our evening meal consists of a pipe of tobacco and a glass of water. A ham was sold for seven dollars. A pound of tobacco cost four dollars. A pound of coffee one dollar. The men have long been without rum. From hard service, and such want, diseases were more and more engendered."*

But that state of want was suddenly changed to superabundance. A British cruiser captured in the gulf a number of merchant vessels loaded with supplies, embracing "rum, meal, coffee, sugar and other welcome provisions," and another exclusively with powder.† Not long afterwards a more brilliant, although not as useful, a prize was captured. It contained $20,000 in coin, a large collection of silver-plate, fine wines, "all sorts of utensils for the kitchen and things of the same kind, being General

---
* Von Elking, Vol. II., p. 146.
† Id. 147.

Galvez's outfit and requirements" for his intended campaign of 1781.* Fortune thus feasted and gilded the victim for the coming sacrifice.

Having perfected the defenses of Fort George, General Campbell turned his attention to Red Cliff, in which, on November 19, he placed a small garrison of 50 Waldecks, under the command of Major Pentzel, at the same time providing it with some heavy artillery, which could be spared from Fort George.

Apparently, tired of waiting for Galvez's attack, or presuming from his delay in making a movement that he had abandoned the intention of attacking Pensacola, General Campbell sent an expedition against a Spanish post, on or near the Mississippi, called French Town by the British. The force consisted of 100 infantry of the Sixtieth regiment, and 60 Waldeckers, besides 300 Indians, commanded by Colonel Hanxleden, the senior officer of the Waldecks, and next in command to General Campbell. It was an unfortunate enterprise,

---

* Von Elking, Vol. II., p. 149.

resulting in the death of the gallant Hanxleden, as well as other veteran officers and soldiers who were soon to be greatly needed at Pensacola. In the retreat, the body of their brave commander was borne by his men from the field of battle to a large oak in its vicinity under the shade of which it was buried. Gratefully did the Waldecks, on their return to Germany, remember and record the chivalric conduct of "the gallant Spaniards who honored fallen gallantry by enclosing the grave with a railing."* On January 9 the remnant of the expedition reached Fort George.

On the ninth of March General Campbell's impatient waiting for Galvez was brought to a close. On that day a preconcerted signal of seven guns from the war-ship *Mentor* told the British that the Spaniards were at last approaching for the final struggle for mastery in West Florida.† By 9 o'clock of the next morning, thirty-eight Spanish ships, under Admiral Solana, were lying off the harbor, or landing troops and artillery. During the night a British

---
*Von Elking, Vol. II., p. 148.
†Von Elking, Vol. II., p. 148.

vessel glided out of the harbor with dispatches to the commandant of Jamaica, pleading for reinforcements, which however were not to be had, for the movements of de Grasse on the Atlantic coast required all the attention of the British navy, whilst Cornwallis and Clinton had drawn, or were drawing, there every available man to meet the great American rally.

On March 11, the Spaniards opened fire upon the *Mentor*, then lying in the harbor, from a battery on Santa Rosa island. She replied to the attack until she had received 28 shots from twenty-four pound guns, when she retired nearer the town.

After this affair there were no further movements by the Spaniards until the eighteenth, when a brig and two galleons, taking advantage of a very favorable wind, sailed past the batteries defending the mouth of the harbor, without receiving any perceptible injury. Thinking they might sail up to the town, and find cover from some structures on the beach, General Campbell caused them to be burned down.

On the nineteenth, the entire Spanish fleet, excepting a few vessels, sailed past the batteries, though subjected to a heavy fire from Red Cliff, which lasted for two hours.

Galvez, even after he found himself in possession of the harbor with a fleet of 38 vessels, and a large land force, consisting not only of troops brought directly from Havana, but those also with which he had captured the posts west of the Perdido, sent to Havana for reinforcements; and remained inactive until they reached him on April 16. The reinforcement consisted of eighteen more ships, and an additional land force, with heavy siege artillery.

Whilst awaiting that addition to his strength, a landing was attempted. The attempt was resisted by a body of Indians and a part of the garrison of Fort George with two field pieces of artillery. The Spaniards, taken by surprise, were driven to their boats. In the attack many were killed, and in the confusion of re-embarking others were drowned. On April 22, however, a second and successful attempt to land was made by the invaders, followed by the establishment of camps where batteries were to be erected.

One of the camps, nearer the Fort and the town

than the others, by its temerity invited rebuke.
Accordingly, a surprise for it, to be executed on
the twenty-third, was prepared, but defeated by
a fanatic. On the night of the twenty-second,
a Waldeck private reported to his captain, that
a Waldeck corporal was missing, under circumstances which implied desertion; that the deserter was a Catholic, the only one in the regiment, the rest being Protestant; and that it had
been suspected by his comrades that his fanaticism would lead him, on the first opportunity,
to desert to his co-religionists. That the suspicion was well founded was manifested by the
movements of the enemy the next morning.

The enterprise, however, though arrested, was
not abandoned. The British commander, shrewdly calculating on the improbability in the enemy's conception, that a surprise defeated on the
twenty-third would be attempted on the twenty
fifth, actually executed the movement on the latter day. The attacking force, composed of a part
of the garrison, and a body of Indians, was commanded by the general in person. The Spaniards
were driven from their entrenchments with
considerable loss, and their works hastily de-

stroyed. This proved, however, the last aggressive act of the British. By the twenty-seventh of April, batteries mounted with heavy siege artillery completely invested Fort George.

On the twenty-fourth, the day before the attack on the Spaniards, General Campbell learned for the first time, that Charleston had been captured by General Clinton on the eleventh of May, 1780. We are not informed of the channel through which the information came to him; but as it could not have come by sea, it must have reached him through the Indians, who obtained it, proably, from traders of the Atlantic coast. His ignorance for nearly a year of so important an event impresses us with his isolation, and the courage with which he bore it. The event was duly celebrated in Fort George by an illumination and a discharge of rockets.

CHAPTER XIV.

Fort San Bernardo—Siege of Fort George—Explosion of Magazine—The Capitulation—The March Through the Breach—British Troops Sail from Pensacola to Brooklyn.

THE Spanish operations against Fort George were conducted with extreme caution. What, in the beginning, was one of a circle of intrenchments, developed into a fort as extensive and strong as the former. Like Fort George, it was built of earth and timber. Its position was about one-third of a mile to the northward of the latter. During its construction it was hidden from observation by a dense pine forest and undergrowth, which, after its completion, were cleared to give play to its guns. It was named San Bernardo, for the patron saint of the Spanish commander.

The magnitude of San Bernardo indicated that it must have been constructed for exigencies besides that of assailing the British works.

Galvez probably feared an attack in his rear from the Indians coming to the relief of their allies, or that he might have to encounter a relieving expedition coming by sea. In either event his fortress would be a place of security for his supplies and a rallying point in case of disaster.

The siege was a struggle between two forts, with the advantage to one of them in being supported by intrenchments which with itself formed a circle around its antagonist. The latter began the contest.

Among the works constructed by the British to strengthen their position, was a redoubt, named Waldeck. On April 27, a Spanish intrenchment was seen to be in the course of construction opposite to Waldeck, under cover of the woods. Against that intrenchment the besieged directed a heavy fire, but with little effect, as the work was nearly completed when discovered. This attack upon the besiegers was the signal for all their batteries to open fire upon Fort George and its defenses.

The firing was incessant on both sides until May 1, when that of the British was almost entirely suspended, for the purpose of enabling the garrison to make some indispensable repairs on their works. On the second, however, the British guns were again in full play.

But the demand for repairs was so continuous and urgent as to impose a heavy tax upon the limited numbers of the besieged. Short reliefs from duty became a stern necessity, and want of rest, as well as overexertion, so impaired their strength that men were seen falling prostrate beside their guns from fatigue and exhaustion.

Galvez's failure to storm the British works, during the silence of their guns on May 1, seemed to indicate his determination to reduce the contest to the question, how long the ammunition of the besieged would last and their artillery remain serviceable? He may, however, have regarded the suspension of the British firing as a strategem to invite an assault.

There was a vital spot in the defenses for which the Spanish shot and shell had been vainly seeking—the powder magazine. But as the gunners were without requisite information to enable them to procure its range, it was but a wild chance that a shell would strike it. That its position was not drawn from the Waldeck corporal, is an impeachment of the military sagacity of the Spanish officers, and an act of gross negligence which would have prolonged the siege indefinitely, but for an imprudence of the British commander equally as gross.

A provincial colonel for infamous conduct—of what character we are uninformed—was drummed out of the Fort, instead of being, as prudence required, carefully kept within it during the siege. The man, as should have been expected, went to the Spaniards and informed them of the condition of the garrison and defenses, and especially of the angle in which the magazine was situated. That disclosure sealed the fate of Fort George. Thenceforward, that angle became the mark of every Spanish shot and shell. For three days and nights did those searching missiles beat upon it, until at last on the morning of May 8, there occurred an explosion that shook Gage Hill to its deep foundations as though once again in the throes of an earthquake.

A yawning breach was made in the Fort.

Fifty men were killed outright and as many more wounded fatally and otherwise.

At that thunder-like signal 15,000 men are marshalled for the assault. But there is no panic in Fort George. Calmly the British commander orders every gun to be charged, and many to be moved so as to sweep the breach. That work done, he hoists a white flag and sends an officer under another to the Spanish general with a communication, which doubtless had been prepared in anticipation of the conjuncture in which he at last found himself. It was an offer to capitulate upon the following terms: "The troops to march out at the breach with flying colors and drums beating, each man with six cartridges in his cartridge box; at the distance of 500 paces the arms were to be stacked; the officers to retain their swords; all the troops to be shipped as soon as possible, at the cost of the Spaniards to a British port, to be designated by the British commander, under parole not to serve against Spain or her *allies*, until an equal number of the same rank of Spaniards, or the troops of her allies, were exchanged by Great Britain, and the best care to be taken of the sick and wounded remaining behind, who were to be forwarded as soon as they recovered."

Knowing that those were the terms which the gallant Dickson and Durnford had demanded and obtained at Baton Rouge and Mobile, the spirit in which General Campbell dictated the terms of the capitulation can be readily imagined. To submit to less than had been conceded to his inferior officers would be dishonor.

Galvez answered, that the terms proposed could not be conceded without modification. General Campbell replied that no modification was permissible; adding, that in case they were not conceded he would hold "the Fort to the last man." That bold reply was followed by the consent of Galvez to the capitulation proposed by the British commander.

It would be a grateful task to record humanity or chivalry as the motive for the concession; and it would be the duty of history to assign it, in the absence of facts, inconsistent with such a conclusion. But the victor, by his own confession, has precluded such a presumption.* In a

---
*Sparks, Vol. 8, p. 175.

letter of General Washington's to Don Francisco Rendon, agent of the Spanish government in the United States, written at "Headquarters before Yorktown, twelfth of October, 1781," occurs the following: "I am obliged by the extract of General Galvez's letter to Count de Grasse, explaining at large *the necessity* he was under of granting the terms of capitulation to the garrison at Pensacola, which the commandant *required*. I have no doubt, from General Galvez's well known attachment to the cause of America, that he would have refused the articles, which have been deemed exceptionable, had there not been very powerful reasons to induce his acceptance of them."

What, it may be asked, were "those very powerful reasons?" He had an army at his command only one thousand less in number than General Washington had before Yorktown, when he wrote the letter to Rendon; he had ample supplies of every description; he was backed by a powerful fleet; he had selected for his expedition a time when de Grasse's movements on the Atlantic coast required the presence, in that quarter, of the whole

British naval force on this side of the Atlantic; and hence, we can find no "necessity he was under of granting terms," which General Campbell "required," unless we find it in his want of faith in his ability by force of arms, to compel the British commander to modify his requirements.

In order to fully appreciate the transaction, it should be borne in mind that there was an understanding between Galvez and the French commanders in America, that he should not grant to British troops that might fall into his power during his operations in West Florida, such terms as would enable them to become a part of the armies operating against the United States.

This understanding Galvez violated at Baton Rouge and Mobile, and again for the third time, in conceding the terms demanded by General Campbell; for the articles bound the garrison not to serve against Spain and *her allies* only, and the United States was not her ally, but only a sympathizer.

To say that the "powerful reasons," to quote from General Washington, were not in Fort

George, would be to accuse Galvez of bad faith to his French ally, and untruth, as to the existence of any necessity for his concession to the British.

Such being the conclusions that impartial history must draw, impressive was the spectacle presented, on the ninth of May, 1781, upon that hill now crowned by the monument to the Confederate dead. In a circle around Fort George the Spanish army stands in array. The roll of a drum breaks the stillness, followed by the sound of mustering in the Fort. Again as it beats to the fife's stirring military air, the British commander, in the dress of a major-general, sword in hand, emerges from the breach, followed by his less than eight hundred heroes. Proudly does the gallant band step the five hundred paces; then successively come the orders to halt, fall into line, and stack arms.

The scene would have thrilled the heart of every soldier whose memory is consecrated by the shaft that springs from that historic hill, then the centre of a landscape, whence, northward, the eye could rest on a limitless expanse of verdure; eastward and westward upon the far-sweeping curves of the shore; southward upon the glorious mirror of the Bay, with the hills of Santa Rosa rising out of the blue waters like snow-clad peaks above the azure of a distant horizon, and far beyond them upon the tremulous sky-line of the heaving gulf.

The formal signing of the articles of capitulation in the Council Chamber of Fort George, which occurred on the ninth of May, immediately before the British marched out, was anticipated in a former page.

On June the fourth the British troops sailed for Havana, where they arrived on the fourteenth of the same month; and thence the same vessels transported them to Brooklyn. A further addition was made to the strength of the British, by the garrisons of Baton Rouge and Fort Charlotte, which after many obstacles, and several voyages from point to point, finally reached Brooklyn about the time the Pensacola troops arrived there. And thus, in consequence of Galvez's breach of faith, a force of 1,200 veterans, with their gallant officers, was added to the British army.

It was doubtless this accession of British

strength, at New York, in that rallying year, when each side required every available man, that caused de Grasse to complain to the Spanish government of the capitulation at Pensacola, and called forth the apology of Galvez referred to by General Washington in his letter to Rendon.

CHAPTER XV.

Political Aspect of the Capitulation—Treaty of Versailles—
English Exodus—Widow of the White House.

THE terms of the surrender of Fort George, as stated in the previous chapter, present the strictly military side of the capitulation. But there was also a political aspect to the formal articles, signed on the ninth of May, by General Campbell, Governor Chester, and General Galvez. West Florida was surrendered to Spain, and it was stipulated, that "the British inhabitants, or those who may have been subjects of the King of Great Britain in said countries, may retire in full security, and may sell their estates, and remove their effects as well as their persons; the time limited for their emigration being fixed at the space of eighteen months."

It was that political feature of the capitulation which made Governor Chester's signature necessary, and to that it related exclusively.

That of General Campbell referred to the strictly military stipulations only. In the former we may find one of General Galvez's inducements to submit to the British general's "requirements."

The object of the Spanish government in directing the invasion of West Florida was to permanently regain the territory which Spain had surrendered to Great Britain in 1763; and in addition, to obtain that part of Louisiana on the Gulf of Mexico which the latter had acquired from France. Consequently, the large expedition so long in preparing against Pensacola, and so disproportionate to the mere capture of the place, was intended for colonization, as well as conquest. Such being the policy of his government, Galvez necessarily subordinated all other considerations to its achievement. Accordingly, his overwhelming numbers designed to overawe opposition; his ponderous siege artillery intended to batter Fort George into ruins without danger to the town; avoidance of all movements by his fleet against it as well as all injury to it by his artillery during the siege; and, lastly, the article above quoted pointed to the colonization of a Spanish population, for the accommodation of which the English homes were to be vacated, and their inmates forced into exile. If that object could be obtained by the capitulation, there was nothing within the lines of Spanish policy to be gained by taking Fort George by storm, at the fearful sacrifice of human life which it would have cost. The French might, indeed, complain that the agreement with them respecting British troops in Florida was violated by conceding the terms demanded by General Campbell; but diplomacy, the science of excuses and pretexts, would be equal to the task of satisfying them. As to the Americans, it was of little consequence to Spain that General Clinton's forces would be strengthened by the reinforcement of the Florida troops, albeit at a conjuncture when every available man was required to sustain Britain's tottering North American empire. For though Spain became an ally of France in order to place herself in a position to claim a fragment of that empire when it fell, yet her purpose was to attain that end with the least possible inconvenience or sacrifice to herself.

That General Washington was satisfied with the apology of Galvez made through de Grasse may well be doubted. His dignity, however, forbade complaint. Besides, the promise violated was made to the French; if they were satisfied, respect for them imposed silence upon the Americans. But there is in the paragraph of the letter to Rendon, before quoted, a vein of irony, the sting of which, coming from such a man, Galvez must have keenly felt.

As already intimated, the above quoted provision of the capitulation became substantially the Fifth Article of the treaty between Great Britain and Spain, signed on the twenty-eighth of January, 1783, at Versailles.*

The condition in which that treaty placed the Florida-English was peculiar. Spain was not opposed to foreigners living in her colonies, provided they were Catholics; and it was well understood, that any English who were, or should become, such would be at liberty to remain in Florida in the full enjoyment of their liberty and property.†

---
*White's Recopilacion, Vol. II., p.298.
†White's Recopilacion, Vol. II., p. 301.

History does not afford a more striking contrast between the conduct of two nations under similar circumstances, to the honor of one, and the reproach of the other, than that between Spain and Great Britain, as they are presented by the treaties of Paris and Versailles. In the former, Spanish subjects were secured in their persons, religion, liberty and property. In the latter, Great Britain virtually stipulated for the banishment of hers, and the confiscation of their estates. The privilege of selling their property within eighteen months was but a mockery; for purchasers were not only few, but well aware, likewise, that a trifling consideration would in the end be preferable to a total sacrifice.

The British government professed to compensate the victims of her policy; but her justice was confined to those whose claims upon it were the slightest; to the absentees owning large tracts of land which had been granted by the crown, and who did not see fit to go to the provinces to attempt to effect sales. *But no indemnity was provided for those who had

---

*Id. p. 300.

made their homes in the provinces, under the gilded representations and inviting promises of their governors in the name of His Protestant Majesty, George III., Defender of the Faith.

The conduct of Spain in this matter is hardly censurable, when it is remembered that it occurred in an age of religious intolerance. She was a Catholic power and wanted no Protestant subjects. Her own had left Florida in 1763, as soon as the Spanish flag was lowered. In the articles of capitulation and the treaty of 1783 she had enforced her traditional policy. And to her credit, be it said, that she did not enforce banishment and confiscation after eighteen months had expired under the former; and when that period had elapsed under the latter, she granted an extension of four months. Great Britain, on the other hand, in yielding to Spain's demands was false to her faith, false to her traditions, and false to that boasted principle of her constitution that her ægis covers every Englishman, in every land.

Eighteen months is but a fleeting span to a people, when it is but a respite from confiscation and exile, avoidable only by apostasy.

Of the heartaches of the exodus of the Florida-English we have an illustration in the widow of the White House. She had lived out the eighteen months under the capitulation, and the like period under the treaty, when the extension came to her like a respite to the condemned.

Those four months embraced the days and nights of her struggle in the toils of temptation, foreshadowed in a previous page. Can she leave that home, consecrated by the graves of her husband and her child; that home where every object, tree, vine, shrub, sea, sky, and the very wild violets at her feet, brought up hallowed associations and sacred memories which made them all parts of her very being? No! The surrender would be at the cost of as many bleeding heart strings. There is, however, an escape in apostasy. She has but to signify her wish to renounce her faith; that faith, however, with which she had consoled a dying husband, and in which she had buried a darling child. Home triumphs. The governor is notified.

Time wanes to the day of sacrifice. The bell tolls the sacrificial hour. The priest stands at the altar ready for the offering. But the victim fails the tryst. Faith triumphs. The bonds of temptation are snapped. Turning her back upon home, she goes forth an exile; crowned, we may well believe, with the promise to all the true of every creed who leave "lands" and "houses" for His name's sake, to swell the mighty host of woman martyrs; time's woeful harvest of blighted lives and broken hearts; victims of man's ambitions, his wars, his policies, and his laws.

CHAPTER XVI.

Boundary Lines—William Panton and Spain—Indian Trade
—Indian Ponies and Traders—Business of Panton,
Leslie & Co.

THE treaty of Versailles re-adjusted the broken circle of Spain's empire on the shores of the Gulf of Mexico, by restoring to it the segment taken from it by d'Iberville's settlement, as well as that cut from it by the Treaty of Paris in 1763.

But British West Florida was not in its entirety acquired by Spain. By the Treaty of Paris of the third day of September, 1783, acknowledging the independence of the United States, the 31° parallel of north latitude was made the southern limit of the latter from the Mississippi river to the Appalachicola. Thence the boundary line was that river up to the Flint, thence in a straight line to the head waters of the St. Mary's and down that river to the Atlantic ocean. The

Treaty of Versailles, on the other hand, made that line the northern boundary of the territory ceded to Spain. Those treaties therefore cut off a huge slice from British West Florida.

But, even within that narrow strip of territory, Pensacola lost its primacy; for in the establishment of the Spanish colonial governments within it, the Perdido was made the western limit of West Florida. Pensacola was, therefore, by that arrangement placed geographically in reference to boundary lines as it stands to-day; the result, as before shown, of d'Arriola having made his settlement three years before the advent of d'Iberville to the gulf coast.

Those territorial changes dealt a withering blow to Pensacola. Instead of being the capital of a province, bounded by the Mississippi and the Chattahoochee, and a line from one to the other some miles north of Montgomery, it became but the chief town of a narrow strip of wilderness between the Perdido and the Appalachicola rivers. Lately regarded and fostered as the future commercial base on the gulf of Britain's North American empire, it now became a garrison town, valued by Spain as only an outpost to guard against encroachments by other powers on the shores of a sea over which she sought supremacy.

Left to Spanish influences exclusively, it must have rapidly dwindled to the condition, commercially at least, in which Captain Wills found it in 1763. But from that fate it was saved by two men who have already been introduced to the reader.

The narrow religious prejudices of the Spanish court demanded the banishment of all Protestant British under the Fifth Article of the Treaty of Versailles; and they were rigidly obeyed by colonial officials with one exception. They knew that to banish William Panton was to insure for the town the fate above indicated, and they were equally aware that his presence would be more effective in the preservation of the peace of the provinces than a large military force, owing to his influence over Alexander McGillivray, and of the latter's over the powerful Creek Indians. Indeed, it is unquestionable, that without those influences, the Spanish government could not have been maintained in West Florida. But it would have been idle to hope that a man who had been loyal to an earthly monarch, under pain of confiscation and banishment, would incur the guilt of apostasy from a faith that was to him, at least, the symbol of allegiance to the King of Kings. Accordingly, the religious test was waived as to him, and for it was substituted an oath of allegiance to the Spanish King, whilst his residence and influence were secured by means the most inviting to his interest and flattering to his pride.

A treaty was entered into with him, as a quasi-sovereign, securing his firm in all its possessions and rights, and bestowing upon its houses at Pensacola, Mobile and Appalachee a monopoly of the Indian trade. For these concessions the firm became the financial agent of the government at those points, and bound to wield its influence in promoting peace and good will between the Spaniards and the Indians.

The stipulations on both sides were faithfully fulfilled. At one time Spain was indebted to the firm in the sum of $200,000 for advances, and the debt was afterwards faithfully discharged. In humiliating contrast with the honor and fidelity which marked the dealings of the Scotchmen and Spaniards with each other, is the following advice of an American agent, James Seagraves, *to his government. "I think if the Spanish court were pushed in the business they will readily sacrifice Panton & Co., especially as they owe the concern $200,000 for Indian supplies."

This advice was given at a time when complications had arisen between the Spanish government of Florida and the United States, growing out of the energetic struggle of the Atlantic Indian traders to divert the Creek trade from Pensacola to Charleston and Savannah. The step suggested was, in effect, to transfer a commercial contest from the Indian wilds to Madrid, where an American minister was expected to perform the degrading task of attempting to induce the Spanish court to commit a fraud upon agents who had served it so long and faithfully, as well as to violate all its other obligations to them.

Panton, Leslie & Co. were engaged in that trade at Charleston and Savannah long before

---

*American State Papers, Vol. III. p. 311.

the American revolution; a trade which, even then, extended through the Coosa country in the heart of the Creek nation. With a full knowledge of it, in all its details, they established themselves at Pensacola with a view of drawing a part of it there. This was the beginning of the commercial struggle which is continued to this day, between the gulf and Atlantic ports for the trade of Central Alabama. It began with the Indian ponies as a means of transportation; it is carried on now by the steam horse; and a future generation may see it continued by electricity.

The pony used by the trader was a strong, hardy little creature, which with ease carried one hundred and eighty pounds and traveled twenty-five miles a day. The rich and abundant pasturage in those times enabled him to supply himself with sufficient food at noon and at night to meet his requirements. There was often oddity in his load. It might be a miniature chickenhouse, or two kegs of taffi, hung to his sides, with a pack of merchandise on his back; or two pendant firkins of honey-comb, with a pile of hides, skins, or beeswax towering between.

One driver for ten animals was the usual proportion of man and beast. The companies were generally from five to ten, making a long line of march, following the main and lateral trails mentioned in a previous chapter. But as all the Indian settlements were visited, their movements could not always be on the ridge. Sometimes creeks and rivers had to be crossed. On such occasions, when the stream was not fordable with safety to the packs, they were ferried over on rafts composed of logs or masses of matted cane, guided where the current was strong by a grapevine rope stretched across the stream.

Regarded by their savage customers as friends, who came periodically to administer to their wants, and gratify their taste for taffi, the traders made their journeys in perfect security. Like their class everywhere, they were joyous men, full of fun and jokes, news and gossip, to which full play was given, under the spur of a cup of taffi, when caravans met.

Beside the trade thus carried on, there was one

equally as great, if not greater, carried on by the Indians themselves, without the intervention of the traders. The business required Panton, Leslie & Co. to keep up a stock of $50,000 at least, and a large corps of clerks to wait on their savage customers.

Other business sprung up and brought population. Sawmills were erected, brickyards opened and a tanyard established, which added leather to the exports of the town.

Such were the fruits of William Panton's presence in the province. Idle, however, would have been his labor, his wealth and talents, though backed by the Spanish Government, but for the co-operation of McGillivray. Had the great Chief pointed his long, slender finger to Savannah and Charleston as the sources of supply for his people, the commercial life of Pensacola would have withered and perished like a tree girdled by the woodman's axe.

CHAPTER XVII.

Lineage of Alexander McGillivray—His Education—Made Grand Chief—His Connection with Milfort—His Relations with William Panton—His Administration of Creek Affairs—Appointed Colonel by the British—Treaty with Spain—Commissioned Colonel by the Spanish—Invited to New York by Washington—Treaty—Commissioned a Brigadier-General by the United States—His Sister, Sophia Durant—His Trials—His Death at Pensacola.

THE people who have been called Creeks in previous pages, received that name after their settlement in Alabama and Georgia; a name, it is said, they derived from the number and beauty of the streams or creeks of the country they inhabited. Before that they were known as Muscogees according to English, and Othomis or Otomies, according to Castilian orthography.

Their original seat was in northern Mexico. They were a warlike and independent tribe, which, though lacking the comparative civilization of the Aztecs and the Tlascalans, had yet received some rays of its light. They had been confederates of the latter in their conflicts for existence with the former. They had afterwards aided in the defence of Tlascala against Cortez. Surviving warriors, however, carried back to their people such accounts of that field of slaughter, and the prowess of the foe, who seemed to be armed with supernatural weapons, that the tribe became panic-stricken, and in a council, resolved upon a flight beyond the reach of the invincible invader. The determination was promptly put into execution.

The entire tribe, bearing off its movable effects, took its line of march in an easterly course. After a journey which consumed many months, they found themselves on the head waters of Red river. Reaching that river, and following it, they at length found a suitable place for a settlement, where they felt they were sufficiently remote from the terrible foe who had inspired their flight. There they accordingly established themselves, and remained for several years. Abandoning that settlement, they proceeded northward to the Missouri, thence to the Mississipi, and from there moved to the Ohio. That progress, however, was not by a continuous march, but by periodic advances, interrupted by settlements more or less long, and marked by conflicts with other tribes, in which, according to their traditions, they were always victorious.

They must have been living on the banks of the Ohio, when Soto made his devastating march through the Creek country which was afterwards to be their home. There they must have been likewise, when de Luna made his explorations, and noted the sparseness of population, and abandoned fields as before narrated; or, perhaps, they were then making one of their intermittent advances southward, which were to bring them eventually to the Coosa, Tallapoosa, and Chattahoochee.

Like other Mexican tribes, the Muscogees were divided into septs or fratries, the most notable of them being those of the Ho-tal-gee, or the Wind, the Tiger, the Bear, and the Eagle. In the first, however, resided the primacy, or hegemony of the tribe.

The traditions of their Mexican origin and emigration, collected by Le Clerc Milfort under the most favorable conditions, as will be seen hereafter, are fortified by their form of government, with its dual executive for civil and military affairs; their glimmer of civilization, as well as their federative tendency.

Soon after their settlement in the Creek country, they are found absorbing other tribes; not by enslavement or incorporation, but as confederates. They had their national councils, composed of the principal chiefs of the confederacy, and suitable buildings at fixed places for their accommodation. The head of the confederacy for civil affairs was the Grand Chief, as the Tustenuggee, or Great Warrior, was for war. They also had Town Governments, the Chief of each being the Micco, an elective officer, and not a King, as often misrepresented. Each town had its council house, in which local affairs were administered.

The Grand Chief of the Muscogees held the position, and exercised the functions which recent criticism has assigned to Montezuma, as the head of the Aztec confederacy, to whom the Spaniards erroneously gave the title, and attributed the powers of an emperor, in accordance with their own habits of thought, as the subjects of an emperor.

The Indian trade that existed between the Creeks and the Atlantic coast, which has already been mentioned, was an inviting field to cupidity and enterprise, and many were the young adventurers from the old world who engaged in it soon after their landing at Charleston or Savannah. Some of them, too, fascinated by the wild life of the forest, made themselves homes in the Creek nation, and found wives amongst the Creek maidens, who in form, feature and habits, were superior to those of other tribes.

Amongst those adventurous spirits was Lachlan McGillivray, a youth of good Scotch family, of Dumglass, Scotland. A few years found him a successful trader. On one of his visits to the Hickory Ground, a prominent Creek town on the Coosa, situated near the present site of Wetumpka, Alabama, he became acquainted with Sehoy Marchand, a young woman whose mother was a full blood of the Hotal-gee, or Wind family, and whose father was a

French captain who had been murdered by mutineers at Fort Toulouse, a few miles from Hickory Ground. That meeting resulted in marriage. Shortly afterward, McGillivray made a home, and established a trading house, not far from where he had first met his Indian wife.

Of that marriage, Alexander McGillivray was the first born, Sophia the next, and Jenette the third.

The father became exceedingly prosperous, partly in consequence of his alliance with the chief family of the Creeks, and in a few years found himself the owner of two plantations on the Savannah river. His trading journeys, however, still had their attractions for him. When Alexander was fourteen years old he induced his wife to let the boy go with him to Charleston, and remain there to be educated. After having been instructed sufficiently for the purpose, he was placed in a counting-house; but having acquired a taste for learning, that occupation became intolerable to him. His father, accordingly, determined to yield to the bent of the boy's mind, and found him a highly educated teacher in a clergyman of Charleston.

With that assistance, and sedulous application, he became a Greek and Latin scholar, and besides, made rapid and extensive progress in other departments of knowledge. He appears to have been a student up to the age of thirty, which he reached about the year 1776. In that year he left Charleston, an educated man, to return to his people, whom he, a little semi-savage of fourteen, had left sixteen years before. The impelling motive to that movement probably was, that being like his father, a loyalist, residence in a rebel colony was no longer agreeable. Possibly, however, he had purposely deferred his return to the Indian nation until he had arrived at such an age as would justify him in looking to the position of Grand Chief. But, be that as it may, the time for his return was judiciously chosen, and consistently with that sagacity which characterized his whole life, of acting opportunely in all exigencies.

The white settlers of Georgia were beginning to press through what the Creeks claimed as their frontier; and to that pressure was added the hostility engendered by the revolution, now in its second year, against any semblance of favor to the enemies of the patriotic cause. The West Florida-English and their government were on the most friendly terms with the Creeks; and that in itself was sufficient to beget hostility to the latter on the part of the Whigs of Georgia and the Carolinas. This was a new and complex condition of things to the Creeks, presenting questions for solution with which their great council felt its inability to deal. To whom could they look for guidance? They knew no disinterested advice could come from the government at Pensacola, and it would be folly to seek counsel from the Georgians, who regarded them as enemies because they desired to be neutrals, living in peace between hostile communities, engaged in a conflict in which the Indian could feel no interest.

It was just at this juncture that Alexander McGillivray found himself amongst his people. Long and impatiently had they awaited the advent of the representative of the Ho-tal-gee, the grand chieftan, who for so many years had been studying that wisdom of the white man, which made him the Indian's superior; that wisdom which now acquired by him, was to be exercised for the salvation of his people. Great, therefore, was the satisfaction produced by the advent of such a disinterested counselor and guide.

He is hardly well within the nation before a grand council is called at Coweta, on the Chattahoochee, over which he was to preside, and formally assume the hegemony of the Hō-tal-gee.

To a thoughtful mind there is a pathos in this scene which appeals to every generous nature! It comes like the despairing appeal of infancy to manhood for help! It is the ignorance of the savage stretching out its supplicating hands to the white man's wisdom as his only refuge.

One of the most striking powers which McGillivray possessed, was his ability to win and retain the childlike confidence of his people, and thereby exercise boundless control over them. He was not a soldier, or a man of blood, in any sense of the term. He was essentially a statesman and a diplomat. The conquests of peace only had any fascination for him. His ambition was to save and civilize his people. That such a man should bend to his will in the paths of peace a numerous population of warlike savages, to whom the war-whoop was music, and scalping the most inviting pastime, is a domination over brute instincts of which history contains very few examples.

A remarkable instance of that influence occurred shortly after the council at Coweta. He there made the acquaintance of Le Clerc Milfort, mentioned in a previous page; an adventurous Frenchman, highly educated, and possessing military qualities of no ordinary kind, as well as bodily strength and endurance equal to any exertion. Their mental culture was a mutual attraction.

Milfort went with him from Coweta to Hickory Ground, the home of McGillivray's childhood, where his mother and his sisters Sophia and Jenette were living. He at once entered into Creek life, and united his fortunes with McGillivray's. The bright eyes of Jenette were not long in winning Milfort's heart, nor was there much delay in his winning hers. They were married. By the marriage he acquired great consideration amongst the Creeks.

As previously remarked, McGillivray was not a soldier himself; but as a wise ruler, he felt the necessity of having an able commander in war, when the exigency for it arose. Moreover, his policy as a civilized ruler, was to have war conducted by a civilized leader, who might by his example and influence, control the brutal instincts of his savage forces. Milfort was the man for the place. An obstacle to his appointment, seemingly insuperable, however, existed. The office of Tustenuggee was an honor to which the Indian braves looked as the highest attainable; and presumptively, they would refuse their consent that this coveted prize should be conferred upon a stranger. But, that stranger had married a Ho-tal-gee, and it was the wish of the Grand Chief that he should receive it. It was, accordingly, conferred upon Milfort with the sanction of the tribe.

McGillivray soon attracted the attention of the British government at Pensacola, as well as that of the British officers in Georgia, with whom he carried on an extensive correspondence. They at once saw that it would be impossible for him to keep the Creeks in a state of neutrality, founded, as it must be, upon good feeling for each of two bitter foes, marked by such strict impartiality of conduct as to avoid any ground of exception by either belligerent. McGillivray's judgment soon led him to the same conclusion; a conclusion which imposed upon him the necessity of choosing one of the belligerents for the ally of his people. He, accordingly, decided in favor of a British alliance, for which the reasons were too obvious for hesitation.

The Americans could reach his people upon one frontier only, and even then their attention would be distracted by their contest with the British. The British, on the other hand, could without danger of interference, assail the Creeks from Pensacola; and in case they crushed, the Georgians would be at liberty to attack them from the east. But, although he sided with the British, it was with the secret resolution that the alliance should be maintained at the least possible sacrifice to his people. His policy was, not to permit their spirit to be broken, or their numbers diminished, by entering with their full strength into a conflict with which they had no concern. Nor would he permit them to inflict such extensive injuries upon Georgia as would be a barrier to future reconciliation.

In order to spur the Creeks to great efforts against the Americans, Tait, a British colonel, was stationed on the Coosa; and at the same time McGillivray received from the British government the commission and pay of colonel in its service. But both expedients proved ineffectual to materially change the policy the latter had adopted. Raids, it is true, were made upon the Georgians, necessarily attended by some blood-shed and rapine, but they were limited in number, character, and consequence, by the mental reservation with which McGillivray had entered into the British alliance. With that limited exertion, however, the British were fain to be content, as it was better for them than strict neutrality, and still more so than the hostility of such a powerful tribe directed against themselves.

Milfort was the commander intrusted with the expeditions against the Georgia settlements; and, doubtless, being fully aware of the conservative policy of the Grand Chief, he made every effort to observe it. A Frenchman, of his ability, was the very man to make such a show of warfare as would impose on the British, and at the same time to render it so barren in results as to make but a transient impression upon those against whom it was directed. That a man should have been selected so eminently qualified to execute such a singular task, affords the highest evidence of the capacity of the mind that made the selection. Such ability, is, indeed, after all, the surest test of the capacity of a ruler.

Though a band of the Creeks, as already mentioned, assisted the British at the time of Galvez's operations against Pensacola, it is remarkable, that neither McGillivray, who was a colonel in the British army, nor Milfort, the Great War Chief, seem to have taken any part in the contest. Such a force as could have been raised by the Creeks and their confederate tribes, could have rendered great service to the British in resisting, if not, indeed, in defeating Galvez's invasion. But an explanation is readily found in the Grand Chief's policy of preventing his people from taking any large part in the quarrels and conflicts of the whites.

Besides, he was doubtless impressed with the smallness of the British force in West-Florida, compared with the host the Spaniards had at their command; justifying the conclusion, that as the latter had been able to conquer the country west, they would prove equal to the conquest of that east of the Perdido. He, therefore, wisely refrained from such an interference as would array the Spaniards against his people, after they had expelled the British from the country. If the British proved victorious, the assistance rendered by the Creeks, aided by the Choctaws and Chickasaws, could be urged as the fulfillment of the obligations of an ally. On the other hand, if the Spaniards were successful, it was an easy matter to disavow the action of an adventurer like Bowles, at the head of a handful of Creeks and other Indians, as one in which the tribe had no concern; an explanation the more acceptable, as the conqueror would naturally seek to cultivate the like friendly relations with the Indians which the conquered had enjoyed.

Soon after McGillivray became Grand Chief of his tribe, he met William Panton at Pensacola. Panton was deeply impressed with his ability. It is probable, too, that he was acquainted with the elder McGillivray, and sympathized with him as a fellow victim, who, like himself, had suffered banishment and confiscation, for no other crime than loyalty to their King. That sympathy with the parent naturally inspired good will toward the son. But, aside from such a sentimental consideration, each soon discovering the great advantage he could be to the other, it was not long before they were united by the more practical bonds of mutual interests. McGillivray likewise saw great advantages to his people in dealing exclusively with a house of such great wealth and influence as that of Panton, Leslie & Co., whilst Panton was as quick to see, that by the management of the Grand Chief the firm could secure a monopoly of the entire Indian trade. It was immediately after this understanding between them was reached, that they had that meeting with Governor Chester in the Council Chamber of Fort George, of which a glimpse was had in a previous page.

The war in Georgia and South Carolina had

cut off the Creek trade with the Atlantic coast; and consequently, McGillivray had no difficulty in directing the whole of it to Pensacola. But after peace was established, the Atlantic traders were again ready, with their pack ponies, to take the trails that led to western Georgia and eastern Alabama. Panton at once saw that the monopoly of his house was in danger; and that to avert it, he must bring about an understanding between the Spanish government, himself, and McGillivray, like that which he had previously effected with the British. He, accordingly, entered into the treaty with the Spaniards, of which mention was made in the previous chapter. To be effective, however, he knew that treaty must be supplemented by another between the Indians and the Spaniards.

In playing his cards, Panton was looking solely to the advantage of his house. But it was far otherwise with McGillivray. If he induced his people to make such a treaty, it was because he saw clearly it was to their advantage. He rejoiced, too, to find that he was about to reap the fruit of that policy by which he had brought them through the period of the

Revolutionary War, stronger, and more numerous than they ever were before; a condition which excited the fears of the Spaniards, and disposed them to seek the alliance of such a powerful tribe by liberal concessions. Accordingly, a treaty between the Creeks and the Seminoles represented by McGillivray, and Spain by Governor Miro of New Orleans, assisted by O'Niell, Governor of West-Florida, and Don Martin Navarro, Intendent General of Florida, was entered into on the first of June, 1784, at Pensacola.* The relations created by that treaty between the Indians and Spaniards were close and intimate, and seem to have been observed substantially, although not always in form, up to the last day of Spanish rule in Florida.

Its conclusion was followed by McGillivray obtaining a commission with the pay of Colonel in the Spanish army.

By that treaty he felt, as he had reason to feel, that he had secured for his tribe an alliance with a strong European power, one that had

---

* American State Papers, Vol. 10, pp. 223-227.

just expelled the British from the Floridas; and, that thus fortified, he was in a condition to meet the Americans on the eastern frontier in a manner that would prevent their threatened encroachment upon the rights of his people; not by war, however, in which the Creeks were to engage with the United States, for such a course, his judgment told him, would end in their destruction. His treaty with the Spaniards was but a card which he proposed to use, to give his nation the imposing aspect of one to be courted rather than despised. To render its attitude still more imposing, he announced his determination to prevent any further encroachments by the whites upon the Indian territory in Georgia.

These cards won the game, according to the calculations of the sagacious brain which conceived it. The United States met the threatening aspect of affairs in Georgia, by appointing commissioners in 1785, to treat with the Indians. One of them, Andrew Pickens, addressed a letter to McGillivray, expressing the wish of the government amicably "to adjust matters on an equitable footing." This was the point for the attainment of which the treaty with the Spaniards, and the threats of hostility against the Georgians had been made. For it was the strength of the Creeks, which his policy had so successfully fostered in the midst of war, backed by the Spanish alliance, that induced the United States, exhausted by the Revolutionary struggle, to resort to peaceable means to avoid a conflict with such a powerful tribe.

The reply of McGillivray so clearly illustrates his profound policy, which previous pages have endeavored to unfold as the moving spring of all his actions as Grand Chief, that it must be given in extenso, especially as any attempt to present it by extracts would prove a mutilation in which its force would be impaired, if not destroyed.

LITTLE TALLASEE, 5th Sept., 1785.

SIR:—I am favored with your letter by Brandon, who, after detaining it near a month, sent it by an Indian, a few days ago. He, perhaps, had some reasons for keeping himself from this region.

The notification you have sent us is agreeable to our wishes, as the meeting is intended for the desirable purpose of adjusting and settling matters, on an equitable footing, between the United States and the Indian nations. At the same time, I cannot avoid expressing my surprise that a measure of this nature should have been so long delayed, on your part. When we found that the American Independence was confirmed by the peace, we expected that the new government would soon have taken some steps to make up the differences that subsisted between them and the Indians during the war; to have taken them under their protection, and confirmed to them their hunting-grounds. Such a course would have reconciled the minds of the Indians and secured the States their friendship, as they considered your people their natural allies. The Georgians, whose particular interest it was to conciliate the friendship of this nation, have acted, in all respects, to the contrary. I am sorry to observe that violence and prejudice have taken the place of good policy and reason, in all their proceedings with us. They attempted to avail themselves of our supposed distressed situation. Their talks to us breathe nothing but vengeance, and, being entirely possessed with the idea, that we were wholly at their mercy, they never once reflected that colonies of a powerful monarch were nearly surrounding us, to whom, in an extremity, we might apply for succor and protection, and who, to answer some ends of their policy, might grant it to us. However, we yet deferred any such proceeding, still expecting that we could bring them to a true sense of their interest; but still finding no alteration in their conduct towards us, we sought the protection of Spain, and treaties of friendship and alliance were mutually entered into—they guaranteeing our hunting-grounds and territory, and granting us a free trade in the ports of the Floridas.

How the boundary and limits between the Spaniards and

the States will be determined a little time will show, as I believe that matter is now on foot. However, we know our limits, and the extent of our hunting-grounds. As a free nation, we have applied, as we had the right to do, for protection, and obtained it. We shall pay no attention to any limits that may prejudice our claims, that were drawn by an American and confirmed by a British negotiator. Yet, notwithstanding we have been obliged to adopt these measures for our preservation, and from real necessity, we sincerely wish to have it in our power to be on the same footing with the States as before the late unhappy war, to effect which is entirely in your power. We want nothing from you but justice. We want our hunting-grounds preserved from encroachments. They have been ours from the beginning of time, and I trust that, with the assistance of our friends, we shall be able to maintain them against every attempt that may be made to take them from us.

Finding our representations to the State of Georgia of no effect, in restraining their encroachments, we thought it proper to call a meeting of the nation, on the subject. We then came to the resolution to send our parties to remove the Georgians and their effects from the lands in question, in the most peaceful manner possible.

Agreeably to your requisition, and to convince you of my sincere desire to restore a good understanding between us, I have taken the necessary steps to prevent any future predatory excursions of my people against any of your settlements. I could wish the people of Cumberland showed an equal good disposition to do what is right. They were certainly the first aggressors, since the peace, and acknowledged it in a written certificate, left at the Indian camp they had plundered.

I have only to add, that we shall meet the commissioners of Congress whenever we shall receive notice, in expectation that every matter of difference will be settled, with that liberality and justice worthy the men who have so gloriously asserted the cause of liberty and independence, and that we shall, in future, consider them as brethren, and defenders of the land.*

I am, with much respect, sir,
Your obedient servant,
ALEXANDER MCGILLIVRAY.

HON. ANDREW PICKENS.

How politic and graceful the allusion to American independence! Could the alliance with Spain have been touched more artfully? How firm is the insistance of the rights of his people! How striking is the regulation of the force exerted in the removal of trespassers from the Indian domain! How worthy of the spring days of republican America is the closing paragraph!

The reader must be induced to read another letter, not merely as illustrative of the style and springs of action of the Grand Chief, but

---

* Indian Affairs, Vol. I., pp. 17-18.

as a narrative of events bearing upon his life, which no pen can so well narrate as his own. It is in reply to a letter of James White, superintendent of the Creek Indians.

LITTLE TALLASEE, 8th April, 1787.

SIR:—It is with real satisfaction, that I learn of your being appointed by Congress, for the laudable purpose of inquiring into and settling the differences that, at present, subsist between our nation and the Georgians. It may be necessary for you to know the cause of these differences, and our discontents, which, perhaps, have never come to the knowledge of the honorable body that sent you to our country.

There are Chiefs of two towns in this nation, who, during the late war, were friendly to the State of Georgia, and had gone, at different times, among those people, and once, after the general peace, to Augusta. They there demanded of them a grant of lands, belonging to and enjoyed as hunting-grounds by the Indians of this nation, in common, on the east of the Oconee river. The Chiefs rejected the demand, on the plea, that these lands were the hunting-grounds of the nation, and could not be granted by two individuals; but, after a few days, a promise was extorted from them, that, on their return to our country, they would use their influence to get a grant confirmed. Upon their return, a general convention was held at Tookabatcha, when these two Chiefs were severely censured, and the

Chiefs of ninety-eight towns agreed upon a talk, to be sent to Savannah, disapproving, in the strongest manner, of the demand made upon their nation, and denying the right of any two of their country to make cession of land, which could only be valid by the unanimous voice of the whole, as joint proprietors in common. Yet these two Chiefs, regardless of the voice of the nation, continued to go to Augusta, and other places within the State. They received presents and made promises; but our customs did not permit us to punish them for the crime. We warned the Georgians of the dangerous consequences that would certainly attend the settling of the lands in question. Our just remonstrances were treated with contempt, and these lands were soon filled with settlers. The nation, justly alarmed at the encroachments, resolved to use force to maintain their rights, yet, being averse to the shedding of the blood of a people whom we would rather consider as friends, we made another effort to awaken in them a sense of justice and equity. But we found, from experience, that entreaty could not prevail, and parties of warriors were sent, to drive off the intruders, but were instructed to shed blood, only, where self-preservation made it necessary.

This was in May, 1786. In October following we were invited by commissioners, of the State of Georgia, to meet them in conference, at the Oconee, professing a sincere desire for an amicable adjustment of our disputes, and pledging their sacred honors for the safety and good treatment of all those who should attend and meet them. It not being convenient for many of us to go to the proposed conference, a few, from motives of curiosity, attended. They were surprised to find an armed body of men, prepared for and professing hostile intentions. Apprehensions for personal safety induced those Chiefs to subscribe to every demand that was asked by the army and its commissioners. Lands were again demanded, and the lives of some of our Chiefs were required, as well as those of some innocent traders, as a sacrifice to appease their anger. Assassins have been employed to effect some part of their atrocious purpose. If I fall by the hand of such, I shall fall the victim of the noblest of causes, that of maintaining the just rights of my country. I aspire to the honest ambition of meriting the appellation of the preserver of my country, equally with the Chiefs among you, whom, from acting on such principles, you have exalted to the highest pitch of glory. And if, after every peaceable mode of obtaining redress of grievances proved fruitless, a recourse to arms to obtain it be a mark of the savage, and not of the soldier, what savages must the Americans be, and how much undeserved applause has your Cincinnatus, your Fabius, obtained. If a war name had been necessary to distinguish that Chief, in such a case, the Man-Killer, the Great Destroyer, would have been the proper appellation.

I had appointed the Cussetas, for all the Chiefs of the Lower Creeks to meet in convention. I shall be down in a few days, when, from your timely arrival, you will meet the Chiefs, and learn their sentiments, and I sincerely hope that the propositions which you shall offer us will be such as we can safely accede to. The talks of the former commissioners, at Galphinton, were much approved of, and your coming from the White Town (seat of Congress) has raised great expectations, that you will remove the principal and almost only cause of our dispute, that is, by securing to us our hunting-grounds and possessions, free from all encroachments. When we meet, we shall talk these matters over.

Meantime, I remain,

With regard, your obedient servant,

ALEXANDER McGILLIVRAY.*

HON. JAMES WHITE.

The foregoing letter illustrates the troubles the Georgians were giving the Creeks, and the call they made upon McGillivray's abilities and influence over his people, in order to avoid a state of war. No result was reached by the Cussetas talk. Matters remained in the same unsatisfactory condition after as before it, and so continued until after General Washington became President of the United States in 1789.

He appointed a new set of commissioners to effect a settlement, but these, like the others, failed to reach a favorable result. On the other hand, their reports were so alarming that he at first regarded war as the only remedy for the troubles existing between the Georgians and the Creeks. But, wisely concluding that the country was not then able to bear the burden of such a costly corrective, he determined to

---

* Indian Affairs, Vol. I., pp. 18-23.

make another effort at conciliation. In this frame of mind the happy thought occurred to him, that a personal interview between him and McGillivray might be attended by results which commissioners had failed to reach. Acting upon it, he sent an agent to the Creek nation, in the person of Colonel Marius Willet, to induce McGillivray to visit New York. The mission was successful. McGillivray in June, 1790, at the head of thirty of the principal chiefs of the confederacy, set out on their long journey mounted on horses.

A stage of the journey brought them to Guildford Court House, where they were honored by a large assembly of the neighborhood. Suddenly the throng around the Great Chief opens to a woman, who rushes up to him, her face bathed in tears, and then, with blessings upon him, expresses her gratitude for a good deed done by him years before, of which she and her children were the beneficiaries. In an Indian raid her husband had been killed, and she and her children carried into captivity. Her benefactor hearing of their melancholy fate redeemed them, and gave them a home in his own house, until an opportunity was afforded of sending them to their friends. He was received with distinguished consideration at Richmond and Fredericksburg. Philadelphia honored him and his company with a three days' entertainment. Colonel Willet, who accompanied them, tells us that upon their landing in New York, the Tammany Society, in full regalia, received them, attended them to Congress Hall, and thence to the residence of General Washington. And then and there, were brought face to face, the most remarkable white man, and the most remarkable red man the western hemisphere had then produced.

Whilst the chiefs of the two confederacies are settling their relations, an interesting event calls our thoughts from New York to Alabama. The impressive influence of the Great Chief's presence was no sooner withdrawn, than a large number of the restless Creeks conceived the purpose of destroying the white settlements on the Tensas, which had been increasing rapidly under his protection. The plan, and the time for its execution were at last fixed. But, fortunately, they were revealed to Mrs. Sophia Durant, the sister of McGillivray.

She possessed remarkable command of the Muscogee language, coupled with the gift of oratory. She often addressed councils at the instance of her brother, who, owing to his long absence from his people in his youth, as well as the study of other tongues, had lost the full command of his own.

At the time she was informed of the bloody scheme, she was at her farm on Little river. Although far under the shadow of maternity she determines, at every risk to herself, by prompt action, to save an unsuspecting population from the terrible fate hanging over them. She orders two horses to be saddled on the instant. She mounts one and her trusty negress the other. More than twice two score human lives depend upon her reaching Hickory Ground in time, and that required a ride of sixty miles. Night and day those two women ride on that errand of mercy. The only pause was when an opportunity offered to summon a chief to the Hickory Ground Council House. The notice flies from chief to chief, that the sister of the

Grand Chief has called a council, to tell them, doubtless, what he had said to her on "talking paper." From all quarters, prompted by interest and curiosity, there is a rush for the Hickory Ground. By that device, worthy the genius of her brother, the council is promptly assembled. She addresses them with a tone of mingled authority and persuasion. She tells them of the scheme that had been disclosed to her; upbraids them for ingratitude to her brother, then with the Great White Chief, who might exact from him and his thirty companions the lives of the murdered whites; warns them, too, of the vengeance which he would be compelled, with the assistance of the whites, to visit upon the murderers; adding all those appeals which in such an exigency would come swelling up from the heart of a noble woman. From all sides of the assembly come pledges that the ringleaders shall be seized, and the enterprise crushed; and promptly and efficiently it was done. History, story and art have commemorated the saving of a single life by Pocahontas; but how insignificant was that act compared with the one just described! The action is further glorified by the fact, that within two weeks after the noble woman had saved so many human beings, she added another life to the long roll of the living.*

A treaty was speedily negotiated between the Creeks and the United States, by which the Oconee lands referred to in the foregoing letter were ceded for an annual payment of fifteen hundred dollars, and a distribution of merchandise. Questions of boundary were settled; the Indian territory was guaranteed against farther encroachment; a permanent peace was provided for; the Creeks and Seminoles placed themselves under the jurisdiction of the United States, and renounced their rights to make treaties with any other nation. All the Indian Chiefs besides McGillivray participated in the negotiation and execution of the treaty.

But besides that open one, there was a secret treaty to which the Grand Chief and the United States only, were parties. It contained a stipulation, that after two years the Indian trade should be turned to points in the United States.

---

*Pickett's History of Alabama, Vol. II. p. 127.

It provided for annual stipends to be paid to designated chiefs. McGillivray himself was appointed Indian agent of the United States, with the rank of a Brigadier-General, and the yearly pay of twelve hundred dollars.*

These treaties were the grounds of severe criticism upon McGillivray. By the open treaty, it was said, he made a surrender of the Oconee country for an inadequate consideration. But the obvious answer to that objection was, that he had exhausted every expedient that his clear and fertile mind could command, to stay the encroachments of the Georgians without a war, an alternative which would have eventually ended in crushing his people. Besides, the plighted faith of the United States, that no farther encroachments should be made upon them, was to them a consideration far exceeding every other; for history had not then declared, as it has since, how frail a barrier against encroachments upon Indian territory is the plighted faith of the nation.

Whatever personal advantages he derived

---

*2 Pickett's History of Alabama, Vol. II. pp. 110-11.

from the secret treaty, whether pecuniary or in dignity, inured to the benefit of his people. To honor him was to give consideration to them; and they regarded the tributes which his abilities drew from the British, the Spaniards, and the Americans, as so many offerings made to the power of the nation. That each of those tributaries complained that he was not their dupe, is alike a proof of his ability, and his fidelity to his people.

For a short time after the New York Treaty he seemed to be losing the confidence of his people, through the machinations of the self-styled General Bowles, who, it will be remembered, assisted with a body of Choctaws, Chickasaws and Creeks, in the defense of Pensacola against Galvez. He was a bold, unprincipled mischief-maker, who would stop at nothing that could be turned to his own advantage; one of those characters who breed suspicion and create confusion for their own profit and consideration. To sap the confidence of the Creeks in their Grand Chief, was to bring about an unsettled condition of things in which he would find himself in his element; and for that purpose he availed himself of the New York Treaty. It would have been an easy matter for McGillivray to have him driven out of the nation, or by the judgment of a council to have taken his life; but neither of these courses suiting his policy, he resolved upon one more subtle and yet as effectual. He visited New Orleans, where it was conjectured he held a consultation with Governor Carondolet, on the subject of ridding the nation of the mischief-maker. Shortly afterwards, Bowles was seized by the Spaniards and sent to Spain. Of the end of his exile we are informed by a letter of General Washington's dated at Mount Vernon, fifth of August, 1793.* "On my way to this place I saw Captain Barney at Baltimore, who had just arrived from Havana. He says, the day before he left that place, advice had been received, and generally believed, that Bowles, who was sent to Spain, had been hanged." Thus ended a chequered life, full of adventures, strange phases, and bad deeds, which it would be interesting to follow were this the proper place.

---

* The same letter speaks of the death of "our friend McGillivray," Sparks, Vol. 10, p. 335.

The New York Treaty was an object of suspicion both to Panton and the Spaniards, although they knew nothing of its secret feature; but they naturally inferred that some other considerations, besides those made public, must have induced the United States to honor McGillivray with the commission and pay of Brigadier-General.

The suspicion, however, resulted profitably to McGillivray. Before he went to New York he complained to Panton of the parsimonious conduct of the Spanish government to him, from whom it expected, and obtained, so much care and labor. Believing this supposed slight on their part was the cause of the favor he manifested for the Americans, that government at once took steps to remove it. He was appointed the Spanish Superintendent-General of the Creek nation, with a salary of two thousand dollars, to which fifteen hundred more were shortly afterwards added.

Soon after McGillivray received that appointment, the Spanish government sent to the Hickory Ground, as its resident agent, Captain Pedro Olivier, accompanied by an interpreter. This man soon became engaged in intrigues to prevent the running of the boundary lines provided for by the New York Treaty; and in this matter he was assisted by William Panton, who visited the Creek nation for that purpose.

This state of things naturally excited the suspicion of the United States, that McGillivray was co-operating with Panton and Olivier. Of any active co-operation by him, however, there is no evidence, as there is none of his active opposition to their machinations. He was too sagacious a man, and had the good of his people too much at heart to engage in the latter. The boundary line fixed by the treaty, had from the first, been exceedingly objectionable to the Creeks, so much so, that even the influence of their Grand Chief had failed to reconcile them to it. Indeed, he himself feared that such a reconciliation was beyond his ability. In self-vindication, in the midst of Olivier's intrigues, he writes to General Knox, Secretary of War: "You recollect, sir, that I had great objection to making the south fork of the Oconee the limit; and when you insisted so much, I candidly told you that it might be made an article, but I would not pledge myself to get it confirmed." It was against the running of that boundary line, that the intrigues of Olivier and Panton were ostensibly directed; but their real object was to keep the Creeks in a ferment in order to exclude their trade from the Atlantic cities, and confine it to Pensacola; the question of boundary being seized upon as a means of accomplishing that end. McGillivray's position was one of great delicacy and responsibility. For him to resist by active opposition those who opposed the running of the boundary line, was not only to do something he had never undertaken to do, but to take a stand that might divide his people into two hostile camps, the most calamitous condition that could befall them.

In the midst of these trials, death came to his relief on the seventeenth of February, 1793, at Pensacola, whilst on a visit to William Panton. He was buried with masonic honors, and, it is said, in Panton's garden. Unfortunately the identity of the spot has defied diligent investigation, and generations have unconsciously desecrated his dust, as they have that of another distinguished man already mentioned. But the suspicion arises that to a different cause must be attributed the oblivion that has befallen the last resting place of the Great Chief, from that which has been assigned in the case of General Bouquet's. Had Panton erected a respectable brick monument even, over the remains of one for whom he professed so much friendship, and who had done so much to increase his fortune, reverently protecting it up to the time he left Florida, this generation might be able to direct the footsteps of the stranger to the tomb of the most remarkable man to whom Alabama ever gave birth, and the most extraordinary man to whom Florida has furnished a grave.

He has been accused of deceit and duplicity in his dealings with the British, the Spaniards and Americans. But truth and candor, if not exotics, are not virile growths in the domain of state craft, while necessity is the ever ready plea on which adepts in the art, or their apologists, rest their vindication. When, therefore, the Great Indian stands condemned at the Bar of Eternal Truth, well may other statesmen and diplomatists whose achievements history delights to record, shrink from the Judgment Seat.

The Grand Chief watched without interference the struggle of the Spanish and British for supremacy in West-Florida, because the true interests of his people pointed to neutrality. Cavour, the ablest and purest statesman of recent times, from a like patriotic motive stood ready, in case of failure, to disavow, the invasion of Naples by Garibaldi, which he had, nevertheless, secretly promoted. If the New York treaty was a gross violation of the Pensacola treaty of 1784, Washington and his cabinet invited, and encouraged, whatever of bad faith there was in the transaction.

The defense of such characters must rest at last upon the final judgment of their own nation upon their life work. So judged, McGillivray is entitled to no low place on the roll of patriotic statesmen.

For seventeen years, dating from the Creek troubles in 1776, up to his death, he had been the guide and shield of his people. For them those were years of comparative peace, growth, and preparation for the white man's civilization, by the example afforded in his own person of its benefits and attractions. With war raging around them, under his guidance, they reached a condition which caused him to be honored, and their alliance sought by two monarchs and a Great Republic. He moved amongst them enjoying the reverence and honor of a patriarchal sheik. Intrigue and detraction brought him under a transient cloud. But when they learned his life was closed in death, their hearts were smitten as those of a family when it loses its head. There went up from the Creek land an universal wail; and again, like a sinister prophecy of evil, there came over it the shadow it was under before the council of Coweta.

Bitter, too, to his people, was the thought, that he slept in the "sands of the Seminoles," and not on the banks of the beautiful Coosa, which he loved so well; where he was born, where he had presided over councils, and made "paper talk" for their good, and where his hospitality was ever ready, alike for the distinguished stranger and the humble wayfarer.

The fate of Milfort may interest the reader. After

the death of McGillivray he returned to France, where in 1802 he published the "Memoire De Mon Sejour Dans La Nation Crëck," to which we owe the preservation of the traditions of that people. But sad to relate, forgetting his Indian wife, he married a French woman. He was made General of Brigade by the Emperor Napoleon. He died in 1814. His French wife was burned to death at an advanced age at Rheims.

CHAPTER XVIII.

Governor Folch—Barrancas—Changes in the Plan of the Town—Ship Pensacola—Disputed Boundaries—Square Ferdinand VII.—English Names of Streets Changed for Spanish Names—Palafox—Saragossa—Reding—Baylen Romana—Alcaniz—Tarragona.

GALVEZ remained but a short time in Pensacola after the surrender of the British. On their departure, he returned to New Orleans, the capital of his province of Louisiana.

In May, 1781, Don Arturo O'Niell was appointed Governor of Spanish West-Florida, and continued to hold the office until 1792. His successor was Enrique White, who was succeeded by Francisco de Paula Gelabert, whose *ad interim* tenure expired in 1796, by the appointment of Vicente Folch y. Juan.

The events of any interest which occurred before that year, have been already mentioned in previous chapters. Folch signalized the early part of his administration by causing a town to be laid out, "between a quarter and half a mile" from San Carlos, that fort having been reconstructed between 1781 and 1796.* This town was officially known as San Carlos de Barrancas, that being the original application to the locality of the Spanish word *barranca*, signifying broken, in the sense in which the term is applied to a landscape.

Folch's purpose in laying out the town was, to substitute it for Pensacola, as the chief town and capital of the province. Of the real motives which prompted the design no information can be obtained. His scheme was defeated, however, by his inability to procure for it the royal approval; the probable result of an appeal to the King by the inhabitants of Pensacola.

He afterwards attempted an important change in the English plan, by laying off into blocks and lots, so much of the park, or public place as is now embraced in the area between Intendencia and Government streets. He also sold many of the lots, which the purchasers proceeded to improve. But, when Intendant Mor-

---

* American State Papers, Public Lands, Vol. IV., p. 136.

ales visited the town in 1806, he utterly disapproved of Folch's proceedings, and refused to confirm the titles of the vendees. Morales' subsequent conduct in the matter, however, shows that in refusing his confirmation he was influenced more by inimical feeling against the governor, than any just sense of public duty, for he himself afterwards granted the lots. This was the beginning of the mutilation of the great public place according to the English plan; a mutilation which was continued from time to time, until there was nothing left but the two small plats of ground known as Seville Square, and that of Ferdinand VII.

His administration in one of its earlier years was marked by one event for which his generation is entitled to credit. A ship of 800 tons was built at *Caranaro*, as the cove in which the Marine Railway is now situated was then known. Her name was Pensacola, and during the decade from 1870, she was still in existence, making voyages to and from Spanish ports. This was the first, and thus far, the last private enterprise of the kind by Pensacolians.

In 1804, the firm of William Panton & Co.,

was dissolved by the death of William Panton, who had been, as we have seen, so prominent a figure in the history of Pensacola, both under the British and Spanish rule. The business of the firm was thenceforward carried on under the style of John Forbes & Co.

In October, 1800, Bonaparte compelled Spain by the treaty of San Ildefonso to cede Louisiana to France; and France, in 1803, sold and ceded it to the United States. The United States, from the time of the purchase, claimed that it extended eastward to the Perdido, which was the eastern boundary of Louisiana in the days of d'Arriola and Iberville, and so remained until the cession, in 1763, to Great Britain of Florida by Spain, and of that portion of Louisiana south of the 31 parallel of N. latitude, east of the Mississippi, by France. The British, after that cession, in creating the province of West-Florida, extended it from the Chattahoochee to the Mississippi. Spain, on the other hand, after the treaty of Versailles, restricted West-Florida to the Perdido, she being at that time the owner of the whole of Louisiana. When, therefore, she ceded Louisiana to France, it was, as claimed by the United States, Louisiana beginning westward of the Perdido; for by contracting the West-Florida of the British, she, to that extent, extended Louisiana to its original limit, and left Pensacola within the boundary line tacitly established by the expeditions of Arriola and Iberville. Spain did not, however, consent to that construction. She claimed that British West-Florida was not embraced in Louisiana; and the question was not finally settled until 1819, when Florida was ceded to the United States. It was, from 1803, up to that cession, a cause of ill feeling and secret hostility on the part of Spanish officials at Pensacola, towards the American settlers in the disputed district.

Folch's official term extended to 1809, and in the number of sovereign masters to whom he was subject during one year of his administration, his official life was remarkable. He was commissioned by Charles IV., who abdicated the throne of Spain in March, 1808. Upon his abdication, his eldest son, the Prince of Asturias, was proclaimed King, under the title of Ferdinand VII. On May 10, Bonaparte, having insidiously enticed Ferdinand to Bayonne, compelled him, by threats against his life, to resign his crown. On June sixth, of the same year, Joseph Bonaparte was proclaimed King of Spain, by no other real authority than the will of his imperial brother.

Never did any event arouse the patriotic resentment of a people, as Spain's was aroused, by the ignominy of witnessing her lawful King deposed, to enable an adventurer to assume his crown. The French Emperor marched army after army into the country, to establish the new dynasty by overawing the people into submission. But army corps led by marshals, whose names had theretofore been the synonyms of victory, only intensified the spirit of resistance. As one man, from the shore of the Mediterranean to the Bay of Biscay, the population flew to arms. Mountain and plain, hill and valley, rang with their battle cry as they hastened to their cities, towns, and villages, to be organized into military commands. The patriotic passion that fired every heart in the Kingdom, was shared by Spaniards in every quarter of the globe. Of the sympathy of Pensacola with the great patriotic movement in the mother country, there exists memorials in the names of some of its streets, and its chief public square.

It was in the fervor of that sympathy that the square received the name of the exiled monarch; a token of loyalty, of which, however, he proved himself unworthy by his conduct after his restoration to the throne. Never had a monarch a better opportunity of making his reign happy and illustrious, and never did one under such conditions make it a source of greater shame to himself, and misery to his people. He was not by nature a cruel, or a bad man; but he was neither firm nor truthful; two weaknesses in a ruler which may prove as fruitful a source of political crimes as a natural inclination to evil actions. In his first proclamation after re-ascending the throne, amid the enthusiastic joy of his people, he said, "I detest, I abhor despotism;" yet he, afterwards, lent himself to schemes which deprived Spain of constitutional government, restored the inquisition, and led to proscriptions involving the lives of some of the patriots who had contributed so largely to the restoration of his crown.

The cruel and despotic policy of his advisers, at length, drove the liberal party into a widespread revolt, which would have resulted in his permanent dethronement, but for the intervention of the French, who, in 1823, enabled him by their arms to keep on his head the crown they had snatched from it in 1808.

But, if in the chief square of the town there be a reminder of a perfidious monarch, there are in some of its streets memorials of Spanish glory.

The English names of those streets were changed to the names they bear, at the time when the events with which the latter are associated occurred, and were designed to be commemorative monuments of the glory shed upon old Spain by the illustrious deeds of her sons. Upon their being monumental, must rest the apology for a slight retracing of their legends, which would otherwise be out of place in this book.

Palafox and Saragossa, or Zaragoza, are the first to arrest attention, as they are likewise suggestive one of the other.

José de Palafox y Melzi, whose ancestral seat

was near the city of Zaragoza, was in 1808, a young officer of the King's guards. He accompanied Ferdinand on his visit to Bayonne, which ended in the King's abdication. It was by him the captive King sent the instructions to the Junta which was to exercise the sovereignty of the Spanish people during the exile of their monarch. Having performed that duty, Palafox went to Zaragoza, to join in the uprising of Aragon, of which it was the capital. Despite his lack of years and experience, his commanding presence led the Aragonese, full of patriotic ardor and warlike impulse, to choose him as their leader, and proclaim him Captain General of Aragon. In a short time he found himself at the head of ten thousand infantry, two hundred horse, and eight pieces of artillery.

Zaragoza, situated on the right bank of the Ebro, was, in 1808, a city of fifty thousand inhabitants. It stood in the midst of an alluvial plain, rich in its olive trees, its vineyards, and agricultural products. Its fortifications consisted of a brick wall not above ten feet high and three in thickness, pierced for guns, but few were in the embrasures. At intervals, however, there were convents, castles, and other solid stone structures. The universal uprising of the Aragonese, and the proximity of the city to the French frontiers, suggested it as one of the most important points for the French to occupy, in the execution of their designs to subjugate Spain. It was, accordingly, one of the first places against which a military force was sent.

In June 1808, Napoleon ordered Lefebvre to advance against it from the Pyrenian frontier. His advance was interrupted by three battles, in which the raw and undisciplined Aragonese peasants did not hesitate to attack the French column, but were in each instance driven back. Lefebvre at last presented himself before Zaragoza, with a demand for its submission. To that demand Palafox made the memorable reply, "War to the knife;" a reply that foreshadowed the terrific struggle by which those old brick walls were to be won by the enemy. In every attack the French made upon the gates and walls, between the twelfth of June and August fifteenth, they were repulsed with fearful loss. Lefebvre, discouraged by his successive failures to carry the place by storm, drew off his army to await the arrival of heavy artillery, to enable him to undertake a regular siege.

The second attempt on Zaragoza began in December, 1808. In the interval between this and the first attack the defences had been greatly strengthened, and a large supply of arms procured. As the French columns advanced towards the city there was presented a spectacle not often witnessed by one doomed to a siege. The entire population, men, women and children, were engaged in the work of preparing for resistance. None left the walls, but on the contrary the peasantry of the surrounding country rushed within them to share in the perilous defence. By the time the French took their position around the city, it had within it fifty thousand defenders, the most of them undisciplined and uninured to arms, yet animated with the spirit of their leader's reply to Lefebvre's demand of surrender.

The French force consisted of two army corps of fifty thousand men, commanded by Marshals Moncey and Montier, with all the necessary artillery and appliances for a siege. For fifty days after the French artillery began to play upon the city the conflict between the besieged and the besiegers was incessant. In that time, thirty-three thousand cannon shot, and sixteen thousand bombs had been hurled against the place. When a breach was made in the wall, immediately and under the terrific fire of the enemy it was closed up with sand bags. If at any point an entry was made within them by the besiegers, the stone houses became citadels for the besieged. If the defenders were driven from a room, a stand was made in the next one. Women and children shared in the labors and the perils of the fight. As a gunner fell at the feet of his wife, stricken down by a cannon shot, she promptly took his place at the gun. Napoleon, dissatisfied with the slow progress made by Moncey and Montier towards a reduction of the place, sent Junot to take the command. Becoming dissatisfied with him, he sent Lannes to bring the operations to a close. Pestilence, too, came to his aid as well as additional forces sent by the Emperor. At last Palafox was confined to his bed with the prevailing epidemic. The French soldiers were at the same time depressed by the fierce and uninterrupted conflict. "Scarce a fourth of the town is won," said one of them, "and we are already exhausted. We shall all perish amongst these ruins, which will become our own tombs, before we can force the last of these fanatics from the last of their dens." With the assailants thus depressed, and the besieged deprived of the presence and encouragement of their leader, besides the havoc of pestilence, a favorable capitulation was accepted by Marshal Lannes. The regular troops marched out of the walls with the honors of war, and were sent as prisoners into France, each soldier retaining his knapsack, the officers their horses and side arms. The peasants were dismissed, and private property was respected. Fifty thousand human beings perished during the siege, all, except six thousand, from pestilence. Palafox remained a prisoner in France until 1814, when he returned to Spain. He was afterwards created Duke of Zaragoza, and died in 1847.

Of this siege a British historian has said: "Modern Europe has not such a memorable siege to recount; and to the end of the world, even after Spain and France have sunk before the waves of time, and all the glories of modern Europe have passed away, it will stand forth in undecaying lustre; a monument of heroic devotion, which will thrill the hearts of the brave and generous throughout every succeeding age."*

Baylen, a parallel street with Palafox, next invites notice. Baylen is a small town at the foot of the Sierra Morena, on the road leading from Cadiz to Cordova and Seville. There, on July nineteenth, 1808, the French General Dupont, after his recent plunder of Cordova, with excesses more in keeping with the days of Alaric, than the nineteenth century, was, with 20,000 men, and all their plunder, compelled to surrender, after a series of battles to a Spanish army, largely made up of irregular Spanish troops.

To Reding, a Swiss in the service of Spain, was due the glory of the event, which excited profound attention throughout Europe, and

---

*Allison's Modern Europe, Vol. III., p. 301.

made a deep and sinister impression on the French.

Of the "catastrophe" Napoleon, who was at Bordeaux when he heard of it, said: "That an army should be beaten, is nothing; it is the daily fate of war and is easily repaired; but that an army should submit to a dishonorable capitulation is a stain upon the glory of our arms which can never be effaced. Wounds inflicted on honor are incurable. The moral effect of this catastrophe will be terrible." Baylen was doubtless the first link in the chain of events which drew from him the reflection in which he indulged at St. Helena: "It was that unhappy war in Spain which ruined me."

Romana street bears the name of the most illustrious General Spain produced during her great Peninsula war—the Marquis de Romana. He was one of those great and generous characters who are too great and generous to be moved by selfishness or envy, and was in consequence the bond of union between the English and Spanish armies. He was marching to the relief of Badajoz, when he was seized with heart disease at Cartaxo, where he died suddenly January 22, 1811. It is enough for his fame for him to have been the subject of the following dispatch by the Duke of Wellington: "In the Marquis de Romana, the Spanish army has lost its brightest ornament, his country its most upright patriot, and the world the most strenuous and zealous defender in the cause in which we are engaged; and I shall always acknowledge with gratitude the assistance which I received from him, as well by his operation, as by his counsel, since he has been joined with the army."

Alcaniz is a reminder of another field of Spanish glory. It is the name of a town in Aragon, on the right bank of the Guadalupe, sixty miles south-east of Zaragoza. It was, on May twenty-third, 1809, the scene of the defeat of a French army under Suchet by the Spanish forces under General Blake.

Tarragona street commemorates one of those sieges like that of Saragossa, which signalize the Spanish race above all others, for the tenacity and devotion with which in all ages it has defended its homes. The city of that name, situated on the Mediterranean shore of Spain, was besieged by Suchet, and defended by General Cortinas, from May 4, to June 29, 1811. The defense was conducted with the same fierce obstinacy and courage which marked that of Saragossa, and with even greater mortality, if allowance is made for the ravages of pestilence in the latter. But there was a vast difference in the finality of the two sieges. Tarragona was taken by assault; and never did American savages exercise more demon-like fury upon unresisting and powerless humanity than the French troops visited upon the Tarragonese. Above six thousand human beings comprising all ages, and both sexes, were massacred whilst appealing for mercy. "The blood of the Spaniards inundated the streets and the houses. Armed and unarmed, men and women, gray hairs and infant innocence, attractive youth and wrinkled age, were alike butchered by the infuriated troops."*

---

* Allison's History of Modern Europe, Vol. III., p. 422.

CHAPTER XIX.

Folch Leaves West Florida—His Successors—War of 1812—Tecumseh's Visit to the Seminoles and Creeks—Consequences—Fort Mims—Percy and Nicholls' Expedition.

In October, 1809, Folch left Pensacola to fill the appointment of Governor of the country west of the Perdido, the capital of which was Mobile. The uneventful period, for Pensacola at least, between that year and 1813, was marked only by the incoming and outgoing of governors. Folch's successor was his son-in-law, Don Francisco Maximiliano de Saint Maxent, under an *ad interim* appointment. In July 1812, he was succeeded by Mauricio Zuniga, who in May, 1813, gave place to Mateo Gurzalez Maurique, whose administration covered the period of the war between the United States and Great Britain, which was declared by the former, on June 18, 1812.

That Pensacola should have been involved in that struggle would seem to be out of the natural order of events, when it is remembered that Spain and the United States were at peace. But, as before intimated, there existed a covert hostility on the part of the Spanish officials at Pensacola against the Americans, growing out of the dispute as to the limits of West Florida; and now intensified by the capture of Mobile on April 13, 1813, by an expedition from New Orleans, under the command of General Wilkinson. Spain herself was too much absorbed by her struggle for existence to take any active interest in a question of boundary in the new world. But the British, who were her allies in her war with the French, availed themselves of that official hostility to induce the Spaniards at Pensacola to permit them to make that place a base from which the Indians could be furnished with supplies to wage war on the United States.

After the capture of Detroit, in August, 1812, the British formed the scheme of combining the Indians on the western frontier of the United States in a line of warfare extending from the

Lakes to the Gulf of Mexico. As their chief emissary to accomplish that end, they employed Tecumseh, the great Shawnee Chief, who in the fall of that year made his appearance amongst the Seminoles and Creeks. He at once began the work of exciting their hostility against the Americans, by every argument, art, and device which his own savage shrewdness could suggest, or the deliberate calculations of his British allies prompt. He addressed the Creek assemblies with the burning words of an impassioned oratory, to which his stately form and commanding presence gave additional force. He upbraided their disposition to adopt the speech, the dress, and habits of the white man, instead of cleaving to those of their forefathers. He persuaded them that it was degrading to an Indian warrior to follow the plow, or to rely upon cattle and the fruits of the field for sustenance; that it was decreed by the Great Spirit that the country should go back to the forest, and that the Indian should depend upon the chase for his food, as his forefathers had done. An invidious contrast was drawn between the disinterested friendship of the British, who had no occasion or use for their lands, and the cupidity of the Americans who were annually restricting their hunting grounds by their ever extending settlements. Superstition, and necromancy, too, were successfully employed to enforce his teachings. Some of the wavering, like Francis, afterwards known as the prophet, were induced to submit to days of seclusion and fasting, in houses from which the light was excluded, until darkness, spells, and incantations, acting upon bodies enfeebled by hunger, inspired faith in the mission of the great Shawnee. A comet, which appeared in the last days of September of that year, was pointed to as a sign placed in the heavens by the Great Spirit, as a presage of wrath and destruction to the white man, and a promise of redemption to the Indian.

He had the temerity, even, to foretell a great natural phenomenon of which he was to be the proximate cause, as an evidence his mission was inspired. "When I reach Detroit I shall stamp my foot, and the earth will tremble and rock." And strange to relate, at about the lapse of time the journey would consume, an earthquake was felt throughout the Creek country, when from all sides came the cry of the awe-stricken Indians: "Tecumseh has reached Detroit and stamped his foot."*

His mission divided the Creeks into two parties, of which by far the most numerous and warlike, was that which yielded to his seductions. To each of his converts he gave a red stick as an emblem of war, and hence the hostile Creeks became known as "Red Sticks."

He had hardly returned to Detroit, when there came to Pensacola British agents, bringing with them military supplies for distribution amongst the Red Sticks, to whose bloody instincts was applied the stimulus of a bounty of five dollars for every American scalp.

That Pensacola should be the Creek base of supply, was in accordance with the plan of warfare designed by the British at Detroit, and a fulfillment of Tecumseh's promised assistance to their savage allies. After the arrival there of the British agents and their stores, the Red Sticks lost no time in procuring from them the needed supplies for the war to which they had

---

* Pickett's History of Alabama, Vol. II., p. 246.

pledged themselves. From all parts of the Creek country the hostiles were seen hurrying to Pensacola, and returning with arms and ammunition, without hindrance from the Spanish officials.

The first startling result of the alliance between the British and Indians, was the massacre of Fort Mims, which occurred in August, 1813, an event that sent a thrill of horror through every American heart.

The fort was situated on Lake Tensas, a mile east of the Alabama river. It consisted of a stockade enclosing about an acre, with a blockhouse in one of its angles. In the center of it stood the residence of Samuel Mims, for whom it was named. It had been hastily constructed, as a refuge for the people of the neighborhood, in anticipation of an extended war, rendered imminent by encounters that had taken place between small parties of Indians and whites. In July, there entered the stockade five hundred and fifty-three souls, composed of soldiers, other men, women and children. Owing to the ill chosen site, situated as it was in a hammock, and the negligence of those in command, the place was surprised at midday on August 30, by one thousand Creek Indians under William Weatherford and Francis, who rushed in at the open gate, which had been heedlessly left unclosed. But few of those in the Fort escaped. All the dead were scalped, except those who were saved from that outrage, by undergoing the process of cremation in the buildings in which they had taken refuge, and which were fired by the enemy to overcome their defenders. Their bloody work finished, the Indians rested and feasted, at the scene of the massacre, smoking their pipes, and trimming and drying the scalps they had taken. Afterwards, these horrid trophies of victory, strung on sticks, were taken to the British agents at Pensacola, who paid for them the promised bounty.

It is due to William Weatherford, who was a son of a half-sister of Alexander McGillivray, that, it should be mentioned, at the peril of his own life, he interfered to save the women and children. Failing in his merciful efforts, he refused to witness their massacre, and left the bloody scene.

Not content with making Pensacola a base

for inciting the Indians to hostitilies against the United States, in 1814, there came into the harbor a British fleet, with a body of marines, the former under the command of Captain William Henry Percy, and the later under that of Lieutenant-Colonel Edward Nicholls, for the purpose of taking possession of its fortifications. This the imbecile Maurique permitted them to do. Fort George, which had been named St. Michael by the Spaniards, resumed its English name, and received a British garrison, whilst the flag of St. George once again floated from its ramparts. Fort San Carlos and the battery on Santa Rosa Island were also turned over to the British. And at the same time, the Governor's house was made the headquarters of Percy and Nicholls.

The fleet consisted of two ships, each of twenty-four guns, and two brigs, each of eighteen guns, with three tenders. The marines numbered two to three hundred men.

Nicholls at once began to increase his force by enlisting Indians, whom he supplied with British uniforms, and drilled in the streets of Pensacola.

Thus reads his order of the day, twenty-sixth of August 1814. "The noble Spanish nation has grieved to see her territories insulted, having been robbed and despoiled of a portion of them while she was overwhelmed with distress, and held down by the chains which a tyrant had imposed on her gloriously struggling for the greatest of all blessings (true liberty). The treacherous Americans, who call themselves free, have attacked her like assassins while she was fallen. But the day of retribution is fast approaching. . . As to the Indians, you are to exhibit to them the most exact discipline, being patterns to these children of nature. You will teach and instruct them, in doing which you will manifest the utmost patience, and you will correct them when they deserve it."

Percy in a communication to Lafitte, the commander of the Banataria pirates, says: "As France and England are now friends, I call on you with your brave followers to enter into the service of Great Britain, in which you shall have the rank of Captain."

Nicholls likewise issued a proclamation to the people of Louisiana and Kentucky, inviting them to join the British. To the latter he addressed himself specially as follows: "Inhabitants of Kentucky, you have too long borne with grievous impositions. The whole brunt of the war has fallen on your brave sons. Be imposed upon no more. Either range yourselves under the standard of your forefathers, or observe a strict neutrality."*

And as an additional stimulus to the activity and zeal of the Indians, the bounty on American scalps was raised from five to ten dollars.†

*Niles' Weekly Register, Vol. VII., pp. 134-135.
†Pickett's History of Alabama, Vol. II., p. 357.

CHAPTER XX.

Attack on Fort Boyer by Percy and Nicholls—Jackson's March on Pensacola in 1814—The Town Captured—Percy and Nicholls Driven Out—Consequences of the War to the Creeks—Don Manuel Gonzalez.

THE first aggressive operation of Percy and Nicholls against the Americans after they had established themselves at Pensacola was an attack on Fort Boyer on Mobile Point, preparatory to an advance on Mobile. But General Jackson's great victory of the Horse Shoe over the Creeks on the twenty-seventh of March had effectually crushed them, and the treaty with them which followed enabled him to direct his attention exclusively to the movements of the British at Pensacola.

His first step was to put Fort Boyer in condition to resist an attack, by repairing it, mounting additional guns and placing an ample garrison in it. This preparation had hardly been accomplished, when, early in September,

1814, the British commanders made a combined attack upon it by land and water. The former was repulsed, and the latter resulted in the destruction of the *Hermes*, Percy's flag ship, and the drawing off of the other vessels in a crippled condition. After the inglorious expedition, the British fleet and land forces retired to Pensacola—a result hardly in keeping with the vaunts of Percy and Nicholls in their several proclamations issued in August.

Pensacola having lost all claim to neutrality, as well by being under the British flag, as by becoming a refuge for the hostile Indians who declined to bring themselves within the terms of the treaty which General Jackson had made with the Creeks after the victory at the Horse Shoe, he resolved to advance upon it. He had previously written Maurique a letter reminding him of the peaceful relations between Spain and the United States, expostulating with him upon his permitting the British to make Pensacola the base of their operations, and allowing it to be an asylum for the hostile Creeks, naming two of them especially, McQueen and Francis, whose strange adventures will be mentioned in a future page. To this mild expostulation the governor made an ambiguous and insulting reply, ending with the threat "that Jackson should hear from him shortly."* The correspondence occurred just before the Percy and Nicholls' attack on Fort Boyer, and doubtless it was their bombastic prediction of success which prompted old Maurique to send Jackson so defiant reply.

General Jackson, however, did not wait longer than the last days of October, 1814, for the execution of the Spanish governor's threat. Having collected his forces at Fort Montgomery, on the twenty-seventh he took up his line of march for Pensacola, the Indian trail referred to in an early chapter being its guiding thread. The troops consisted of the Third, Thirty-nineth and Forty-fourth infantry, Coffee's brigade, a company of Mississippi dragoons and part of a West Tennessee regiment, numbering three thousand effective men, besides a band of friendly Choctaws.

He reached the vicinity of the town on the

---

* Niles' Weekly Register, Vol. VII., p. 11.

evening of the sixth of November. He first appeared on its western side, and there, having halted, he says, in the dispatch containing an account of the expedition, "On my approach I sent Major Pierre with a flag to communicate the object of my visit. He approached the Fort St. George with his flag displayed, and was fired on by the cannon from the fort."* Immediately afterwards, with the adjutant and a small party, he himself made a reconnoissance. He found the fort manned by Spanish as well as English troops. He likewise observed that there were in the harbor seven English war vessels, which it was necessary for him to consider in his future movements. His plans were at once formed. A force under Captain Denkins, with several pieces of artillery, occupied the site of Fort St. Barnardo, which was once again to be pitted against its old antagonist, Fort George.† Inferring that the enemy would expect his attack from the west, General Jackson, on the night of the sixth, caused the main body of his army to make a circuitous march, so that

---

* Niles' Weekly Register, Vol. VII., p. 281.
† Niles' Weekly Register, Vol. VII., p. 281.

the morning would find it on the eastern extremity of the town.* This movement shielded him from the guns of St. George or St. Michael, whilst by entering the town at the eastern end of Government street he would, in a measure, be protected from the guns of the English vessels. But he encountered a battery of two guns as he entered the street, which fired upon the centre column with ball and grape, whilst there opened upon the troops a shower of musketry from houses, fences and gardens.† The battery was soon silenced, however, by a storming party led by Captain Laval, who lost a leg at the last fire of the guns. All the Spanish forces at the battery fled as Laval's command rushed upon it except a gallant Spanish officer, who, refusing to fly, was taken prisoner. But tradition says, instead of laurels, he won from his own people the imputation of "fool" for his rashness—a rashness, however, which, had it been crowned with success, would probably have secured him the praise of a hero.

---

* Niles' Weekly Register, Vol. VII., p. 281.
† Niles' Weekly Register, Vol. VII., p. 281.

When the command had well advanced into the town it was met by the governor in person, with a white flag, and an offer of surrender at discretion. The offer was accepted, but solely for the purpose of enabling General Jackson to accomplish the declared object of the expedition —which was not conquest—but to expel the British, whose presence was due to the imbecility of Maurique, as well as the small Spanish force at his command, consisting, as it did, of two or three companies of the regiment of Tarragona. In order to attain that object, possession of Forts Barrancas and St. Michael by the Americans was indispensable, and, to the extent of his ability, the governor made the surrender. But when Captain Denkins and his command were about to proceed to take possession of St. Michael, Captain Soto, the Spanish officer in command, refused to obey the governor's instructions to make the surrender. Preparations that were immediately made to take it by storm, however, induced Soto to reconsider his refusal and to admit the American command. The demand was made at six o'clock on the evening of the seventh, and the surrender occurred at midnight. The purpose of Soto's delay cannot be divined, for Nicholls having on the night of the sixth withdrawn his men to the shipping, there remained in the fort but a small band of Spaniards.

As General Jackson withdrew his forces from the town, which he did on the evening of the same day of its capture, they were fired upon by the British vessels, but without inflicting any injury.

Whilst, on the morning of the eighth, a detachment was preparing to march on Barrancas, with the purpose of cutting off the retreat of the British fleet, there was heard a great explosion, which it was at once concluded was occasioned by the blowing up of San Carlos. General Jackson nevertheless sent the detachment there to verify the fact. On its return in the night it reported the fort blown up, everything combustible burned, and cannon spiked by the British, who had taken to their ships, and sailed out of the harbor.

The only casualties which occurred doing these operations on the part of the Americans were seven killed and eleven wounded, including

Captain Laval; and on the part of the Spaniards four killed and six wounded.

Captain William Laval was a South Carolinian, the son of a French officer of the Legion of Lauzun, belonging to the French forces in the Revolutionary war. In 1808 he received the commission of ensign in the American army. In 1812, he became a first lieutenant. The breaking out of the Creek war found him a captain. He was with the third regiment, to which his company belonged, at the battle of Holy Ground. For the service of charging the Spanish battery at Pensacola he was specially selected by General Jackson. The loss of his leg prevented his sharing with his regiment in the glorious victory of New Orleans, and ended his military career as well. His aptitude for civil as well as military life was manifested by his filling the offices of Secretary of State, Comptroller General, and Treasurer of South Carolina, as well as Assistant Treasurer of the United States under Polk's administration.

That the presence of the British was enforced, and by no means agreeable to the Spaniards, was promptly manifested by the good feeling exhibited by the latter towards the Americans, as soon as Percy and Nicholls had taken their departure. The inhabitants were much impressed by the kind and generous conduct of General Jackson; who seems fully, to have appreciated the peculiar position in which the town was placed, by the pretentious audacity of Percy and Nicholls, the feebleness of its garrison, and above all the imbecility of Maurique. In the dispatch before referred to he says: "The good order and conduct of my troops, whilst in Pensacola, have convinced the Spaniards of our friendship and our prowess; and have drawn from the citizens an expression, that 'The Choctaws are more civilized than the British.'" In letters written from Pensacola to Havana, in relation to the capture of the place, the comparison is thus expressed: "the American Choctaws were more civilized than the religious English." These letters teem with the praises of the considerate conduct of General Jackson and his army.

When the first account of the invasion reached Havana, American vessels were seized as a retaliatory measure; but when all the particulars of the expedition were learned they were promptly released.

Having blown up St. Michael, General Jackson left Pensacola, on November 9, to go to the defence of New Orleans, which from all indications was threatened with an attack by the British. There he arrived with his army, on December 2, to begin those preparations which were to end on January 8, in the grand and glorious land victory of the War of 1812.

When Percy and Nicholls left Pensacola, they took with them, not only their Indian allies, but also about one hundred negro slaves belonging to the inhabitants of the town. Sailing to Appalachicola, they there landed the Indians and negroes. Still bent on instigating a savage warfare against the American settlements, a fort under their directions was built on the Appalachicola river, which they supplied with guns and ammunition. It was designed to serve as a refuge for fugitive slaves, and a resort for hostile Indians, as well as a salient point from which to carry on an exterminating warfare against the white settlements in southern Georgia and Alabama.

Such were the inglorious results of the Percy-Nicholls expedition to Florida, beginning, as we have seen, with stilted proclamations to the people of Louisiana and Kentucky, coupled with an invitation to a nest of pirates to become their allies; and ending with the robbing and destruction of the property of a community to which they had come under the guise of friendship, and as its shield from wrongs which existed in their own imaginations only.

Aside from the barbarity which marked the warfare instigated by Britain against the Americans in Florida and Alabama during the years 1812-1814, history has cause to lament its fatal consequences to the people who were the cruel instruments by which it was waged.

At the time of Tecumseh's mission to the Creeks, about twenty years had elapsed since the death of their Great Chief, McGillivray. In that interval, under the impulse of his teachings and example, continued and increased by the fostering care of the United States, they had made considerable advance in civilization. Large numbers of them had learned to rely more upon tillage and their herds for a livelihood,

than on the chase. It was no uncommon thing
to see in the nation, well-built houses standing
in the midst of considerable farms. They owned
slaves and large herds of cattle. The hum of
the spinning wheel, and the noise of the shuttle,
moved by the deft hands of Indian matrons,
were common sounds throughout the Creek
country; whilst an Indian maiden with her
milk pail, or at her churn, was no unusual sight.
The schools established amongst them were
gradually shedding upon them the light and
mellowing influence of knowledge.*

The large infusion of white blood into the
tribe, owing to the attractions of the Creek
women, which have already been noticed, likewise, added the hope of a civilization resting
upon the strongest instincts of human nature.
Of the possibility of this civilizing and ennob-
ling influence, gradually permeating and elevat-
ing the Creeks as a people, we have the evidence
in some of their descendants, who at this day,
are amongst the most respectable citizens in
several communities in Alabama and Florida.

---

*Niles' Weekly Register, Vol. 6, p. 370.

Such was the state of the Creek nation, when the British at Detroit sent Tecumseh, like another Prince of Evil, into that fair garden of a nascent civilization, to convert its peaceful scenes into fields of slaughter, with all the woes that follow in the footsteps of war.

The first fruit of that cruel scheme, as we have seen, was the tragedy of Fort Mims. Then followed in rapid succession the avenging battles of Tallasehatchee, Talladega, Auttose, and Holy Ground. To those succeeded the last great heroic struggle at the Horse Shoe, in which, of one thousand Red Sticks engaged, two hundred only survived. Afterwards came the surrender of Weatherford with that speech *

---

* Weatherford having boldly ridden up to General Jackson's tent, was met by the threatening question: "How dare you, sir, ride up to my tent after having murdered the women and children at Fort Mims?" Weatherford replied: "General Jackson, I am not afraid of you. I fear no man, for I am a Creek warrior. I have nothing to request in behalf of myself; you can kill me if you wish. I come to beg you to send for the women and children of the war party who are now starving in the woods. Their fields and cribs have been destroyed by your people, who have driven them to the woods without one ear of corn. I hope you will send

which comes to us as the dirge-like epilogue of the woeful drama; and a memorial of that prophetic shadow which fell on his people when they learned their Grand Chief was lying in the "sands of the Seminoles."

The Spaniards criticised General Jackson's Florida campaign, because he did not, instead of advancing on Pensacola, proceed at once to Barrancas, to capture San Carlos, and thereby prevent the escape of the British vessels. But the answer to the criticism is, that he was not aware, perhaps, of all the conditions known to the Spaniards, which in their judgment, would have facilitated a surprise, or contributed to a successful assault. Besides, such a movement would have been inconsistent with the purpose of his invasion, which was to procure the exclusion of the British from Florida, by the

---

out parties to safely bring them here in order that they may be fed. I exerted myself in vain to prevent the massacre of the women and children at Fort Mims. I am now done fighting. The Red Sticks are nearly all killed. If I could fight you any longer I would most heartily do so. Send for the women and children; they never did you any harm. But kill me if the white people want it done."—Pickett's History of Alabama, Vol. II., p. 349.

action of the Spaniards themselves; a consideration which was due to the amicable relations existing between Spain and the United States. Entertaining these views, General Jackson did not deem it proper to seize the Spanish forts in the first instance without communicating with the Governor. This he attempted to do, and it was only after the outrage of firing on his flag, he resolved, without further parley or remonstrance, by his own arms to drive out the British.

That, however, he had considered a movement on Barrancas, before or at the time of his advance on Pensacola, is evidenced by an interview which he had with Don Manuel Gonzalez, who was an officer in the Spanish commissary department, and who had a cattle ranch at a place then known as Vacaria Baja, now as Oakfield, one mile from the trail the American army was following. Don Manuel, with his family, was at the ranch, when the General rode up to the house, and accosted him. There was with the Don at the time, his son, Celestino, then a young man. Through an interpreter, the General made known, that the purpose of his visit was to require the Don, or his son, to guide the army to Barrancas. The Don boldly refusing, the General became insistent, to the degree of threatening the use of force to secure compliance. Roused by the threat, with a mien as dauntless as Jackson's, Don Manuel replied: "General, my life and my property are in your power; you can take both; but my honor is in my own keeping. As to my son, I would rather plunge a sword into his bosom than see him a traitor to his king." The General replied by extending his hand with the exclamation, "I honor a brave man," and thenceforth became his friend.

CHAPTER XXI.

Seminole War, 1818—Jackson Invades East Florida—Defeats the Seminoles—Captures St. Marks—Arbuthnot and Ambrister—Prophet Francis—His Daughter.

AT the close of the war between the United States and Great Britain, the British troops were withdrawn from the fort on the Appalachicola river built under the auspices of Nicholls and Percy.

The Seminoles were, as their name signifies, outlaws and runaways from the Creek confederacy, or their descendants. Hence it was, that those of the Red Sticks who refused to submit to the terms of the treaty between the United States and the Creeks, either fled to the British at Pensacola, or to the Seminole nation. It was in a district inhabited by Seminoles, that the fort built by Nicholls on the Appalachicola river was situated. The spirit and objects which prompted its construction continued to animate its motley garrison long after Nicholls' departure. At length it proved such an interruption to navigation, besides being an asylum for runaway negroes, as to bring against it, in 1816, an expedition by land and water under Colonel Duncan L. Clinch. A shot from a gunboat exploded the magazines and destroyed the larger part of the garrison. The destruction of this nest of rapine, however, did not for long give peace and security to the district.

In the fall of 1817, a feeling of unrest and suspicion mutually seized upon the white settlers and Indians, induced by causes for which both were responsible. The first act of war, however, was the capture on November 21 of Fowlton, a Seminole village above the Georgia line, by an American force, under Colonel Twiggs. This proved the signal for Indian massacres, the most shocking of which was that of Lieutenant Scott and his command. Whilst going up the Appalachicola river in a barge they were attacked from a dense swamp on the bank. There were in the barge forty men besides Scott, seven soldiers' wives, and five children. All were killed except one woman spared by the Indians, and four men who swam to the opposite bank.

In March 1818, General Jackson was ordered to the seat of war. He invaded East Florida, and in a campaign of six weeks crushed the Indians. In one of their towns, were found three hundred scalps of men, women and children, fifty still fresh hanging from a red war pole. He also captured the Spanish Post of Saint Marks.

For the last act, investigation can find no adequate reason. It was not, however, an irremediable wrong, for restitution furnished a remedy. Two irreparable wrongs, however, marked that short campaign.

Alexander Arbuthnot, being found at St. Marks, was brought before a court-martial. He was a man of seventy years of age, a Scotchman, an Indian trader, and a friend of the Indians, but a counsellor of peace between them and the whites; a man of education, who used his pen to represent Indian wrongs to both Spanish and American officials; and who, when Jackson was about to invade their country, advised the Seminoles to fly and not to fight. On his trial, the plainest rules of evidence were disregarded, and without proof he was found guilty of the charges of inciting the Creeks to war on the United States and, likewise, of "aiding and abetting the enemy, and supplying them with the means of war." Under that baseless judgment the old man was hanged; his waving white locks protesting his innocence.*

Robert C. Ambrister, who had formerly belonged to Nicholls' command, being found in the Indian nation, was also seized and tried by a court-martial. He confessed that he had counselled and aided the Indians. The court at first sentenced him to be shot, but before closing the trial, upon a reconsideration it set aside that judgment, and substituted for death the punishment of fifty stripes, and confinement "with a ball and chain at hard labor for twelve months." Nevertheless, General Jackson disregarding the last, executed the first judgment.†

Jackson having early in May closed his campaign against the East Florida Seminoles, and obtained evidence satisfactory to himself,

---
*Niles' Weekly Register, Vol. 15, pp. 270—282.
†Niles' Weekly Register, Vol. 15, p. 281.

that the Spanish officials at Pensacola were in sympathy with them, resolved to march upon that town, and repeat the lesson which he had taught it in 1814. Before following him in that expedition, however, mention will be made of the adventures, fate and daughter of Francis, the Indian prophet, who left Pensacola, it will be remembered, with Nicholls on the approach of the Americans in 1814.

Francis had been one of Tecumseh's most notable and zealous disciples, as well as one of the most sedulous in making Red Stick converts. A leader in the massacre of Fort Mims, he had revelled in deeds of blood in that human slaughter pen. When Nicholls left Florida with his troops, Francis accompanied him, and finally made his way to London. There in a gorgeous dress he was presented to the Prince Regent, who in recognition of his military services to the crown, bestowed upon him a gilded tomahawk, with a dazzling belt, a gold snuffbox, and a commission of brigadier-general in the British service. Well would it have been for the prophet had he remained in a land where his deeds were so highly appreciated. But the instinct of the savage brought him back to Florida, where he was captured by the decoy of an American vessel lying in the St. Marks river, flying a British flag. He went off to her in a canoe, to meet allies, but found enemies, who seized and delivered him to Jackson. He was summarily hanged, with his brigadier's commission on his person.

It is a pleasing change to turn from deeds of blood to instances of humanity, especially when they come to us in the form of attractive youth. A young Georgian, named Duncan McRimmon, captured by the Indians whilst he was fishing, was doomed to death. The stake was fixed, the victim bound, the faggots and torch were ready, when a deliverer came in the person of Milly or Malee, a girl of sixteen years, the daughter of Francis. Her intercessions induced her father to spare McRimmon and send him to St. Marks to insure his safety. Not thinking himself secure there, McRimmon went aboard the decoy vessel, and by a singular fatality was there when Francis also came.

Malee, bewitching in face, slender and graceful in form, a Red Stick in blood and courage, an expert with the rifle, a fearless rider who required no other help than one of her small hands to mount, was the ideal of an Indian heroine. She was likewise sprightly in mind, and spoke English and Spanish as well as Indian.

An adventure will illustrate her heroic nature. After her father's capture, but in ignorance of it, she and several attendants barely escaped the snare into which he had fallen. As they approached the decoy, however, something occurring to excite suspicion, their canoe was turned for the land. To arrest it, a blank shot was fired by the vessel. That being unheeded, a charge of grape shot was sent after the fugitives. The missiles fell around them, but the canoe neither pausing nor changing its course, was paddled the faster for the shore. A boat was sent in pursuit, but the chase was too late. As the heroine leaped from the canoe to the beach, she snatched a rifle from an attendant and fired at the pursuers. The ball having grazed several of them, and struck the rudder-post, put an end to the chase.

After the close of the war, McRimmon sought

Malee in marriage. His suit, after repeated refusals, was crowned with success. A marriage, and a happy plantation home on the Suwanee, were the fruits of her humanity, and his persistent wooing. After eighteen years of married life, Malee found herself a widow with eight children.

Among the Red Sticks, who after the disastrous battle of the Horse Shoe fled to the Seminole nation, were a Creek mother and her orphan boy, whose age might be twelve. The young Red Stick was destined in after years to fill the continent with his name. Osceola was old enough at the time of Tecumseh's mission, and the stirring events in which it resulted, to receive from them a deep and lasting impression. To those impressions, doubtless, and the blood he derived from one of those Spartan warriors, whose heroism excited the admiration of their conquerors,* was due his primacy in the

---

*So impressed was General Jackson's chivalric nature with the lion-like courage of the Red Sticks at the battle of the Horse Shoe, that he made an earnest, but ineffectual effort to end the conflict, and thereby save a remnant of that band of heroes.

Seminole war; for an alien he was without the influence of a sept to achieve it. In the career of the Seminole chief may be discerned the far-reaching influence of the Great Shawnee, and the abiding force of youthful impressions.

CHAPTER XXII.

Jackson's Invasion of West Florida in 1818—Masot's Protest — Capture of Pensacola — Capitulation of San Carlos—Provisional Government Established by Jackson—Pensacola Restored to Spain—Governor Callava—Treaty of Cession—Congressional Criticism of Jackson's Conduct.

HITHERTO Jackson's operations had been confined to the province of East Florida. On the tenth of May, 1818, he began his invasion of West Florida by crossing the Appalachicola river at the Indian village of Ochesee. Thence he followed a trail which led him over the natural bridge of the Chipola river—a bridge which it would be difficult for the wayfarer to observe, as it is formed by the stream quietly sinking into a lime-stone cavern, through which it again emerges within a distance of half a mile.

Within a few hundred yards of the trail, and near the north side of the bridge, there is a cave one-fourth of a mile in length, with many lateral grottoes, its roof pendant with glittering stalactites and its floor covered with lime-stones moulded in varied and eccentric forms. Panic-stricken by Jackson's campaign in East Florida, the Indians on the west of the Appalachicola river, when he began his westward march, made this cave a place of refuge, and were there quietly concealed when his troops unconsciously marched over their subterranean retreat.

The army marched in two divisions. The one commanded by Jackson in person followed the bridge trail, the other moved by a trail which led to the river, northward of the place where it made its cavernous descent. The water being high, the construction of a bridge or rafts became necessary to enable the wagons and artillery to cross. Whilst the northern division was thus obstructed, General Jackson, unimpeded in his march, reached the appointed place of junction. Here he waited, in hourly expectation of the appearance of the other column, until worked up to a frenzy of impatience which was changed to indignation when, after the junction, the interposition of a river—contradicted, as he supposed, by his own immediate experience—was assigned as the cause of the delay. At length, however, the guides, by disclosing the existence of the bridge, solved the riddle and restored the general to good humor.

His march westward, and south of the northern boundary of the province of West Florida, brought him to the Escambia river, which, having crossed, he reached the road that he had opened over the old trail in 1814, when he marched to Pensacola on a similar mission to that in which he was now engaged.

Don José Masot, who was governor of West Florida, having received intelligence of Jackson's westward march and his designs on Pensacola, sent him a written protest against his invasion, as an offence against the Spanish king, "exhorting and requiring him to retire from the Province," threatening if he did not, to use force for his expulsion. This protest was delivered by a Spanish officer, on May 23, after Jackson had crossed the Escambia river and was within a few hours' march of Pensacola. Notwithstanding Masot's threat, instead of advancing to meet the invader, he hastily retired with most of his troops to Fort San Carlos, leaving a few only at Pensacola, under the command of Lieutenant-colonel Don Lui Piemas, for the purpose of making a show of resistance.

Masot's protest, instead of retarding, seems to have accelerated Jackson's advance. In the afternoon of the same day on which it was received, the American army was in possession of Fort St. Michael and encamped around it. Thence, immediately upon its occupation, Jackson sent Masot a dispatch in reply to his protest, in which he demanded an immediate surrender of Pensacola and Barrancas. In his answer, on May 24, to that demand, Masot, as to Pensacola, referred Jackson to Don Lui Piemas; as to San Carlos he replied: "This fortress I am resolved to defend to the last extremity. I shall repel force by force, and he who resists aggression can never be considered an aggressor. God preserve your excellency many years." Upon the receipt of this communication, Jackson, by arrangement with Colonel Piemas, took possession of Pensacola.

On the twenty-fifth, Jackson replied to Masot's dispatch of the twenty-fourth, in which he tells him he is aware of the Spanish force, and hints at the folly of resistance to an overwhelming enemy. In conclusion he says: "I applaud your feelings as a soldier in wishing to defend your post, but when resistance is ineffectual and the opposing force overwhelming, the sacrifice of a few brave men is an act of wantonness, for which the commanding officer is accountable to his God."

In the evening of the day on which Jackson's communication was written, and within a few hours after it was received by Masot, Fort San Carlos was invested by the American army. On the night of the twenty-fifth, batteries were established in favorable positions within three hundred and eighty-five yards of the fort, though the work was interrupted by the Spanish guns. Before the American batteries replied, Jackson, in his anxiety to spare the effusion of blood, sent Masot, under a flag of truce, another demand to surrender, accompanied by a representation of the futility, if not the folly, of further resistance. The refusal of the demand was followed by the batteries and the fort opening upon each other. The firing continued until evening, when a flag from the fort invited a parley, which resulted in a truce until the following day, the twenty-seventh, when, at eight o'clock in the morning, articles of capitulation were signed. Such was Masot's defense to "the last extremity," and such the fruit of Jackson's expostulation with his fiery but feeble antagonist.

The military features of the capitulation were that the Spanish surrender should be made with the honors of war, drums beating, and flags flying, during the march from the gate of the fort to the foot of the glacis, where the arms were to be stacked; the garrison to be transported to Havana; and their rights of property, to the last article, strictly respected.

But, as in the case of General Campbell's and Governor Chester's surrender, in 1781, to Galvez, there was a political aspect to the capitulation of Masot.

In Jackson's despatch to Calhoun, Secretary of war, he says of the capitulation: "The articles, with but one condition, amount to a complete cession to the United States, of that portion of the Floridas hitherto under the government of Don José Masot." The condition alluded to was, that the province should be held by the United States until Spain could furnish a sufficient military force to execute the obligations of existing treaties.

Having accepted the cession of West-Florida to the United States, Jackson further assumed the authority of constituting a provisional government for the conquered province. He appointed one of his officers, Colonel King, civil and military governor; he extended the revenue laws of the United States over the country; appointed another of his officers, Captain Gadsden, collector of the port of Pensacola, with authority to enforce those laws; declared what civil laws should be enforced, and provided for the preservation of the archives, as well as for the care and protection of what had been the property of the Spanish crown, but now, in the General's conception, become the property of the United States.

Shortly after these occurrences, General Jackson, with his constitution sorely tried by the fatigue and privations of the campaign, left Pensacola for his home in Tennessee, to find quietude and repose, made sweet by public applause on the one side, and interrupted by bitter censure and criticism on the other.

The views with which Jackson began the Seminole campaign in March, and those which he entertained at its close in May, by the capitulation of Masot, present a strange and striking contrast. He invaded East-Florida to crush the Seminoles, as he had crushed the Creeks of Alabama. This he accomplished by invading the territory of a power at peace with the United States. As an imperious necessity, the invasion was justified by his government. During his operations, however, he acquired information from which he concluded that there existed a sympathy between the Spanish officials at Pensacola and the Indians. Ostensibly, to correct that abuse he marched to Pensacola, where he ended his campaign by procuring the cession of the province of West-Florida, followed by the establishment of an American government, without the authority of the United States.

The United States, without formally disavowing Jackson's conduct, signified its readiness to restore Pensacola and St. Marks whenever a Spanish force presented itself to receive the surrender. In September, 1819, such a force appearing at Pensacola, the town and Barrancas were immediately evacuated by the American troops. And thus ended the government established by Jackson, after it had existed fourteen months, during which it was administered to the satisfaction of the inhabitants of the Province.

With the troops there came as governor Don José Maria Callava, knight of the military order of Hermenegildo, who, in 1811, had won the cross of distinction for gallant conduct in the battle of Almonacid, one of the many fiercely fought battles of the Peninsula war.

The advent of the Spaniards seemed to be inconsistent with the fact that, on the twenty-second of the previous February, a treaty had been entered into between Secretary Adams and Don Louis de Onis, the Spanish minister for the cession of the Floridas. But it was subject to the ratification of both governments, and, though ratified by the United States, it had not been acted upon by Spain. At first the re-occupation might have been considered a matter of form, in which a sensitive government consulted its dignity by placing itself in a condition to make a voluntary surrender of territory for a consideration, instead of appearing to submit to a conquest. But, as time rolled on without a ratification of the treaty by Spain, the re-occupation of Pensacola seemed to point to her determination to permanently retain the Floridas.

It was believed, at the time the treaty was negotiated, that Jackson's bold action had done more to bring it about than Mr. Adams' diplomatic skill, a belief for which there was an apparent foundation in the delay of Spain to ratify it after the pressure of his conquest was removed.

No instance in the life of that great man more strikingly illustrates than these transactions the beneficent working of that imperious will, to which he made everything bend that stood in the way to the attainment of what he conceived a patriotic end.

The necessity for the campaign of 1814, as well as that which he had just closed, convinced him that Florida, as a Spanish colony, would be a constant menace to the peace and security of the border settlements of Alabama and Georgia, not so much from the hostility of the Spanish as their inability to control the restless and war-like Seminoles. He saw, too, the necessity of making Spain sensible of her obligation to exercise the necessary restraint upon her savage subjects, and at the same time to make her fully realize the large and onerous military establishment it would be necessary to maintain in Florida to accomplish that object. The articles of capitulation brought the United States and Spain face to face upon this question. It impressed upon the former the imperative necessity of securing a permanent cession, and it compelled the latter to count the cost involved in fulfilling the condition by which only the provisional cession could be nullified.

A study of the correspondence between Masot and Jackson, whilst the latter was still east of the Appalachicola river, creates the impression that the reason assigned by Jackson for his expedition to Pensacola was but a pretext, and that the real motive was made manifest by the articles of capitulation—a provisional cession, as the first step to a permanent cession. He was unsustained by his government openly, at least, he was censured by a congressional committee and denounced by the press, but he soon found his vindication in public opinion, enlightened by subsequent events.

Masot, the other chief actor in these transactions, had been appointed governor of West Florida in November, 1816, and, as we have seen, his official term ended with the capitulation of the twenty-seventh of May, 1818. Shortly afterwards he left Pensacola for Havana in the cartel *Peggy*, one of the vessels provided by Jackson to carry the Spanish governor to the latter place. The *Peggy* was overhauled by an armed vessel under the "Independent Flag," as the ensign of Spain's revolted South American colonies was called. No lives were taken, nor was the *Peggy* made a prize, for she was an American, but the Spaniards were robbed. Masot had with him eight thousand dollars in coin, which he had concealed. A slight suspension by the neck, however, as a hint of a higher and more fatal one, wrung from him the hiding-place of his treasure, which he lost, but saved his life.* The *Peggy* was overhauled by the "Independent Flag," during a voyage to Havana from Campeachy, whither she had taken refuge from what was supposed to be a piratical vessel.

During Masot's administration there occurred a transaction which occupied a place in the investigations of the special committee of the senate of the United States, appointed, in 1818, to inquire into and report upon the occurrences of the Seminole war of that year, prominent amongst them the capture of St. Marks and Pensacola. The committee condemned all Jackson's proceedings and seem to have even harbored the suspicion that a land speculation prompted him to exact a cession of the latter place. The circumstances which induced the suspicion are detailed in an affidavit of General John B. Eaton, afterwards secretary of war under Jackson and governor of Florida, which appears amongst the documents accompanying the report of the committee.†

---
* Niles' Weekly Register, Vol. XV., p. 261.
† Niles' Weekly Register, Vol. XV., p. 88.

It seems that, in 1817, Eaton and James Jackson of Nashville—nowise related to General Jackson—foreseeing that Florida was to be acquired by the United States, resolved to make a purchase of lots in Pensacola and lands in its vicinity. To them were afterwards added six associates, John McCrae, James Jackson, Jr., John C. McElmore, John Jackson, Thomas Childress and John Donelson, who was a nephew of Mrs. Jackson. Donelson and a Mr. Gordon were appointed to proceed to Pensacola to make the purchases. As a measure of security to Donelson and Gordon, Eaton applied to General Jackson and obtained for them a letter of introduction to Masot. Provided with this letter, which facilitated their operations, Donelson and Gordon went to Pensacola and fulfilled their mission by buying a large number of unimproved town lots, sixty acres of land adjoining the town and a tract on the bay two or three miles to the westward.

Eaton says: General Jackson had no interest in the speculation, nor was he consulted respecting it, his only connection with it being the letter to Masot. As there is no allusion to the transaction in the report of the committee, they must have concluded that the suspicion which prompted the search for evidence respecting it was unfounded. Such at least must be the just conclusion from the silence in respect to the matter observed by a document so full of pointed condemnation of Jackson's acts, of the manner in which his army was raised and the officers commissioned by himself, the executions of Arbuthnot and Ambrister, the capture of St. Marks and Pensacola, the establishment of a provisional government, the extension of the revenue laws of the United States over the conquered province, and the appointments for it of a governor and a collector of the customs.

CHAPTER XXIII.

Treaty Ratified—Jackson Appointed Provisional Governor—Goes to Pensacola—Mrs. Jackson in Pensacola—Change of Flags—Callava Imprisoned—Territorial Government—Governor Duval—First Legislature Meets at Pensacola.

ALTHOUGH the United States was unremitting in its efforts to induce Spain to ratify the treaty of cession, her ratification was postponed from time to time under various pretexts. Prominent English journals having declared, that if Florida was ceded to the United States, Great Britian, in order to maintain her influence in the Gulf of Mexico, should insist upon a surrender to her of the Island of Cuba, public opinion in the United States settled down to the conclusion that the delay of the ratification was due to British intrigue. But, that this opinion was ill founded, is evident from President Monroe's message of the seventh of December, 1819, in which he says: "In the course which the Spanish government has on this occasion thought proper to pursue, it is satisfactory to know that they have not been countenanced by any European power. On the contrary, the opinion and wishes of both France and Great Britain have not been withheld either from the United States or Spain, and have been unequivocal in favor of ratification."

The procrastination of Spain was the occasion of intense public feeling in the United States; which at length formally manifested itself on March 8, 1820, in a resolution reported by the committee of Foreign Relations of the House of Representatives, to authorize the President to take possession of West Florida. Patience, however, prevailed, and on February 19, 1821, the ratification took place.

General Jackson was shortly afterwards appointed Provisional Governor of Florida, and instructed to proceed to Pensacola with a small military force, to receive from the Spanish authorities a formal surrender of West Florida. On April 18, he left the Hermitage, with Mrs. Jackson and his adopted son, Andrew Jackson

Donelson, to enter upon the long, tedious journey to Pensacola, via New Orleans.

A stage of the journey in Southern Alabama, brought him to a military post, in the neighborhood of which, William **Weatherford**, the Creek hero, resided. At the suggestion of General Jackson, Colonel Brooke, the commandant of the Post, and his host, invited Weatherford to dine with his conqueror. The invitation was accepted. When the Great Chief appeared, Jackson cordially met him, and taking him by the hand, presented him to Mrs. Jackson as "the bravest man in his tribe."

Coming into Florida early in July, on reaching what was then known as the Fifteen Mile House, now as Gonzalia, where Mr. Manuel Gonzalez then had his cattle ranch, the General spent several days with him. Whilst there, hearing of the approach of his troops, accompanied by Mr. Gonzalez, he went up the road to meet them. Coming to a creek, they saw the wagons of several up-country traders stuck in the mud, which the latter, for lack of sufficient force, were making ineffectual attempts to move. On the other side of the branch were several men lying on the ground, and horses grazing near them. Accosting the men who were tugging at the wheels of a wagon, Jackson said, "Why don't you get those men across the branch to help you?" "Oh! they say they are General Jackson's staff." "Well," said he, "I am General Jackson himself, and by the eternal, I will help you!" And with those words, dismounting from his horse, and throwing off his coat, he lustily put his shoulder to the wheel.

Upon the arrival of the troops at the Fifteen Mile House, headquarters were established, and remained there until all the arrangements were made for a formal change of government.

Mrs. Jackson, however, took up her residence at Pensacola two or three weeks before July 17, when the change of flags was to take place. During the Sundays which preceded the change, Mrs. Jackson, who was an eminently pious woman, cherishing great reverence for the Sabbath, was greatly scandalized by the manner in which it was dishonored. Shops did more business on that day than any other. It was a day of public gambling, fiddling, dancing, and boisterous conduct. When the last Sunday of

Spanish rule came, seemingly because the last, the fiddling, dancing, noise and confusion, exceeded that of any preceding one. Unable to restrain her pious indignation, Mrs. Jackson vented it in a protest against the Sabattic Saturnalia, made through Major Staunton, with the emphatic announcement that the next Sunday should be differently spent.

In anticipation of the change of government, there was a large influx of people from the States, induced by the great expectations entertained of the future of Pensacola; a future in which it was confidently predicted, it was to be the rival of New Orleans. Many persons also came expecting official appointments from the new Governor, but who, greatly to his chagrin, as we learn from Mrs. Jackson's letters, were disappointed, in consequence of the President himself making the appointments.

At length the sun arose upon the day when its beams were for the last time to bathe in light the ancient banner of Castile and Aragon, as the emblem of the sovereignty of these shores. In the early morning appeared in the Public Square the Spanish Governor's guards, handsomely dressed and equipped, consisting of a full company of dismounted dragoons of the regiment of Tarragona. After a parade, they fell into line south of the flag staff, extending from east to west in front of the Government House, which stood on the north-east corner of Jefferson and Sargossa streets. At eight o'clock there marched down Palafox street a battalion of the Fourth Infantry, and a company of the Fourth United States Artillery, coming from their camp at Galvez Springs, which filing into the Square, formed a line opposite the Spanish guards, and north of the flag staff. Precisely at ten o'clock, General Jackson and his staff, entering the Square, passed amid salutes from the Spanish and American troops, between their lines to the Government House, where Governor Callava awaited him for the purpose of executing the documentary formalities of the cession. As the first sign that this act was performed, the Spanish sergeant guard at the gate was relieved by an American sentinel. General Jackson and Governor Callava then left the house, and passed between the double line of troops. As they reached the flag staff the Spanish flag came down, and the stars and stripes went up, saluted by the Fourth Artillery and the sloop-of-war *Hornet*, whilst her band, assisting at the ceremony, played the Star Spangled Banner.

At Barrancas the ceremony was slightly different. The flags of both nations appeared at the same time at half-mast. In that position they were saluted by the Spaniards. As the flags were separated, one ascending and the other descending, both were honored with a salute by the Americans.

The day was naturally one of rejoicing to the Americans, but as naturally one of sadness and in some instances of heart aches to the Spanish population. The advantages of being under the United States government were too great not to be appreciated by owners of real estate and business men generally. But there was a sentimental side to the change. Some of the Spanish garrison had married in Pensacola, and with others the inhabitants had formed social ties, induced by a common language, habits and tastes. To them it can well be imagined that the change of flags was but the presage of bitter separations. In 1763 all the Spanish left the country, and in a common exile mutual consolation was found; but, in 1821, the sorrow was that a part went and a part remained to mingle with a strange people. Mrs. Jackson, in a letter, thus expresses the emotions of the occasion: "Oh! how they burst into tears to see the last ray of hope depart from their devoted city and country—delivering up the keys of the archives—the vessels lying in the harbor in full view to waft them to their distant port. . . . How did the city sit solitary and mourn. Never did my heart feel more for a people. Being present, I entered immediately into their feelings."

The Sunday following the change was, according to Mrs. Jackson's prediction, one of quietude and freedom from the license of previous ones, which had so shocked her religious sensibilities. She thus expresses the change: "Yesterday I had the happiness of witnessing the truth of what I had said. Great order was observed, the doors kept shut, the gambling houses demolished, fiddling and dancing not heard any more on the Lord's day, cursing not to be heard." For the change the lovers of Sunday quietude were doubtless indebted to Mrs. Jackson, for her prediction is not to be taken as that of a prophetess who merely foresees and foretells, but that of a woman with a will of her own, and conscious of her ability to direct the stern governor in the exercise of his authority, at least outside of politics.

The next morning after the change of flags, the Spanish officers and garrison sailed for Havana in the transports *Anne Maria* and *Tom Shields*, under convoy of the United States sloop-of-war *Hornet*.

Governor Callava and staff, however, remained in Pensacola, where his handsome person, polished manners, soldierly bearing and high character made him a general favorite with the American officers and their families, who extended to him every social courtesy. General and Mrs. Jackson, however, were distant and reserved in their bearing towards him, resulting in some measure from a prejudice against Spanish officials induced by the general's experience with Maurique and Masot. Perhaps, too, there mingled with that prejudice a slight feeling of jealousy of Callava's social success, a weakness from which strong characters, under the insinuation of others, are not exempt.

There soon occurred, however, a painful interruption of the gallant Spaniard's social enjoyment—so graceful an attendant of the change of government—by an occurrence which must be regarded as a lasting reproach to its authors.

The treaty required the Spanish government to surrender all documents relating to private rights in the archives of the province. This duty had been performed by Callava, who had caused a separation to be made between the documents falling within the definition of the treaty and others which did not, and had delivered the former to Alcalde H. M. Brackenridge, an appointee of the American governor. The latter papers, packed in boxes for transportation to Havana, were placed in the custody of Doningo Sousa, one of Callava's subordinates. In the separation of the papers, one relating to the estate of Nicholas Maria Vidal, involving a trifling sum, was by accident placed with the documents in one of the boxes in Sousa's possession.

A woman claiming to be an heir of Vidal complained to Brackenridge that the paper had not been delivered to him and was about to be removed to Havana by Sousa. Brackenridge, instead of politely calling Callava's attention to the woman's complaint and asking for a surrender of the document, at once made a preemptory demand for it upon Sousa. Sousa properly declined compliance, alleging his want of authority to do so without instructions from Callava, and at the same time, to relieve himself from responsibility in the matter, sent the boxes to Callava's house. Brackenridge at once reported the matter to Jackson, who ordered Sousa to be imprisoned, and at the same time Callava to be arrested and brought before him immediately, although it was night and Callava was at the time at a dinner party at Colonel Brooke's. When the knightly Castilian was brought before Jackson, he naturally proposed to enter a protest against such astonishing proceedings. This Jackson would not permit, but insisted that Callava should at once answer interrogatories to be propounded to him. Callava's persistent attempts to protest were as persistently interrupted by Jackson, until at last the latter, in a rage of passion, ordered him to be imprisoned, an order which was promptly executed by commiting him to the calaboose, where Sousa had preceded him. This outrage committed, Alcalde Brackenridge, as if determined to leave no bounds of decency unviolated, had the boxes at Callava's house opened that night and took from one of them the worthless paper—worthless at least to the claimant—that had occasioned the trouble.

For this disgraceful transaction Brackenridge is primarily responsible. He was an intelligent lawyer, afterwards a judge, and later a member of Congress from Pennsylvania; and therefore, presumably acquainted with the decencies, to say nothing of the amenities of official intercourse. He was likewise well acquainted with Jackson's prejudices and irascible temper, as well as what a fire-brand to his nature were the wrongs, whether real or simulated, of a woman. In the light of these considerations, Brackenridge must stand condemned, as either a wilful mischief-maker, or a wily sycophant, playing from selfish motives, upon the weaknesses of a great man.

But neither Jackson's greatness, nor his being the dupe of Brackenridge, can remove from him the reproach of having in this transaction violated official courtesy, the chivalrous consideration due by one distinguished soldier to another, as well as the laws of international comity and hospitality.

A writ of Habeas Corpus was issued by Hon. Elijias Fromentin, U. S. Judge for West Florida, to bring before him Callava and Sousa, on the night they were committed. Obedience to the writ was refused by the guard, who sent it to the Governor. Thereupon, His Excellency issued a notice to the Judge to appear before him, "to show cause why he has attempted to interfere with my authority as Governor of the Floridas, exercising the powers of the Captain-General and Intendant of the Island of Cuba." The Judge prudently delayed his appearance until the next day, in order to allow the Governor time to cool; but in the meantime remained in momentary expectation of a guard to take him to jail. The affair, however, ended in a stormy interview, in which to the Governor's question, whether the Judge "would dare to issue a writ to be served on the Captain-General," the latter replied, "No, but if the case should require it, I would issue one to be served on the President of the United States."

After the troublesome paper was procured by Brackenridge, an order was made for the release of Callava. A few days after his release he left Pensacola for Washington to make his complaints to the United States government.

Some of the Spanish officers whom he had left in Pensacola, published after his departure, a paper expressing their sense of the outrage to which he had been subjected. This being regarded by Jackson as an attempt "to disturb the harmony, peace and good order of the existing government of the Floridas," the protesting Spaniards were by proclamation ordered to leave the country by the third of October, allowing them four days for preparation, "on pain of being dealt with according to law, for contempt and disobedience of this, my proclamation."

A tragedy occurred during Jackson's rule,

which illustrates his lack of tenderness of human life. With full knowledge of the affair, he permitted a duel to be fought in a public place by two young officers, Hull and Randall. When he was informed that the former had fallen, shot through the heart, pistol in hand, with the trigger at half-cock, he angrily exclaimed: "Damn the pistol; by G—d, to think that a brave man should risk his life on a hair-trigger!"

Jackson's bearing generally, and especially his summary dealings with Callava and Sousa, had inspired the population with great fear of his despotic temper. Of that feeling there occurred a ludicrous illustration. An alarm of fire brought a crowd to the Public Square, which was near the fire. General Jackson also hurried to the scene. To stir the lookers-on to exertion, he made a yelling appeal. The crowd not understanding English, and thinking it had heard a notice to disperse, took to its heels, and left the General the sole occupant of the Square.

Mrs. Jackson was a domestic woman, and better satisfied to have her husband at home, than to see him in exalted stations requiring his absence from the Hermitage. Whilst in Pensacola, she pined for that dear spot; and it is, evidently, with joy, that she announced in a letter to a friend, that the General calls his coming to Florida, "a wild goose chase," and that he proposed an early return. In October they returned to Tennessee.

That a man of his estate and political prospects, should have accepted, to fill for a few months, the office of Governor of a wilderness, with a salary of $5,000, admits of only one explanation. His recent campaign had been so severely condemned, that he regarded the tender of the appointment by Mr. Monroe, as having the semblance, at least, of a national apology for the injustice which he had suffered, and accordingly he accepted it in the spirit in which it was tendered. In a word, he filled the office, because filling it would be a vindication of his conduct in the campaign of 1818.

On the third of March, 1822, congress established a territorial government for both the Floridas as one territory. The first governor under the territorial organization was

W. P. Duval of Kentucky, who had represented a district of that state in congress, and who was the original of Washington Irving's Ralph Ringwood. He resided, temporarily, in Pensacola, where the legislative council of thirteen, appointed by the President, held its first session. It had hardly begun its work, however, when the yellow fever breaking out compelled an adjournment to the Fifteen-mile house, before mentioned, where the Florida statutes of 1822 were enacted. One of them illustrates the vice or virtue there may be in a name. The title of "An Act for the Benefit of Insolvent Debtors," was misprinted in the laws of the session so as to read: "An Act for the Relief of Insolent Debtors." The error destroyed its utility, and no man, it is said, as long as it remained on the statute book, ever invoked the relief of its provisions.

The limit assigned to these historical sketches has now been reached. The space that intervenes between the visit of the luckless Navaez to Pensacola bay and the establishment of the territorial government of Florida embraces a period of nearly three hundred years. The changes and shifting scenes which, during that period, marked the history of the settlements on its shores, stand in contrast with the persistency of the arbitrary boundary line of the Perdido, established by the mutual consent of the Spanish and French in the early years of the eighteenth century. Disturbed by the English dominion for twenty years, it was restored by the Spanish, and finally confirmed in 1822 by the act of congress establishing a territorial government for the Floridas.

In 1820 the constitutional convention of Alabama, in anticipation of the ratification of the Spanish treaty, memorialized congress to embrace West Florida within the boundaries of that state. The memorial enforced the measure with all those obvious arguments which come to the mind when it turns to the subject. But they were silenced, as if by the imperious decree of fate that the Perdido boundary should be, and forever remain, a monument of d' Arriola's diligence in reaching the Gulf coast three years before d' Iberville.

www.ingramcontent.com/pod-product-compliance
Lightning Source LLC
Chambersburg PA
CBHW032059220426
43664CB00008B/1060